A

HOPE

MORE

POWERFUL

THAN

THE SEA

A
HOPE
MORE
POWERFUL
THAN
THE SEA

One Refugee's
Incredible Story of
Love, Loss, and Survival

Melissa Fleming

FLATIRON
BOOKS
NEW YORK

The views expressed herein are those of the author and do not necessarily reflect the views of the United Nations.

A HOPE MORE POWERFUL THAN THE SEA. Copyright © 2017 by Melissa Fleming. All rights reserved. Printed in the United States of America. For information, address Flatiron Books, 175 Fifth Avenue, New York, N.Y. 10010.

www.flatironbooks.com

Design by Donna Sinisgalli Noetzel

The Library of Congress Cataloging-in-Publication Data is available upon request.

ISBN 978-1-250-10599-8 (hardcover)
ISBN 978-1-250-10601-8 (e-book)

Our books may be purchased in bulk for promotional, educational, or business use. Please contact your local bookseller or the Macmillan Corporate and Premium Sales Department at 1-800-221-7945, extension 5442, or by e-mail at MacmillanSpecialMarkets@macmillan.com.

First Edition: January 2017

10   9   8   7   6   5   4   3   2   1

To Peter, Alessi, and Danny, my parents,
and the over sixty-five million people who
have been forced to flee from their homes.

Contents

ONE: A Childhood in Syria   1

TWO: The War Begins   21

THREE: The Siege of Daraa   50

FOUR: Life as a Refugee   81

FIVE: Love in Exile   105

SIX: The Engagement   128

SEVEN: Deal with the Devil   143

EIGHT: Ship of Horrors   174

NINE: All That Is Left Is the Sea   191

TEN: Rescue at the Dying Hour   220

Epilogue   253

A Note from Doaa   261

Author's Note   263

Six-year-old Doaa couldn't remember any moment when she'd ever been alone. She lived with her parents and five sisters in a single room in her grandfather's two-story house. Her father's three brothers and their families occupied the other rooms, and each moment of Doaa's life was filled with relatives: She slept side by side with her sisters, ate communal meals, and listened to spirited conversations.

The Al Zamel family lived in Daraa, the largest city in the southwest of Syria, located just a few kilometers from the Jordanian border and about a two-hour drive south of Damascus. Daraa sits on a volcanic plateau of rich, red soil. In 2001 when Doaa was six, it was famous for the bounty of fruits and vegetables the land yielded—pomegranates, figs, apples, olives, and tomatoes. It was said that the produce of Daraa could feed all of Syria.

Years later, in 2007, a devastating drought swept through the country, lasting for three years, and forcing many farmers to abandon their fields and move with their families to cities such as Daraa to seek employment. Some experts believe that this massive displacement gave rise to the ripple of discontent that in 2011 swelled into a tidal wave of protest, and then the armed uprising that would shatter Doaa's life.

But back in 2001, when Doaa was just a little girl, Daraa was a peaceful place where people went about their lives, and newfound hope was held for the future of the country. Bashar al-Assad had just succeeded his repressive father, Hafez al-Assad, as president. The people of Syria were hopeful that better times lay ahead for their country, at first believing that the young president would break away from his father's oppressive policies. Bashar al-Assad and his glamorous wife had been educated in England and their marriage was seen as a merger—he from the minority Alawite branch of Islam and his wife, Asma, like Doaa's family, from the majority Sunni. His politics were secular, and hope was widespread, particularly among the Damascus-educated elite, that under his leadership the forty-eight-year-old emergency law his father had inherited and maintained to crush dissent would be revoked and restraints on freedom of expression would be lifted. Under the pretext of protecting national security from Islamic militants and outside rivals, the government had used its emergency powers to severely restrict individual rights and freedoms and to enable security forces to make preventive arrests with little legal recourse.

The more conservative, poorer populations, such as those in Daraa, mainly hoped for economic improvements, but for the most part they quietly accepted the way things operated in their country. This silent acquiescence was the result of a harsh lesson they had learned back in 1982 in the city of Hama, when then president Hafez al-Assad ordered the killing of thousands of citizens as a collective punishment for the rise of the Muslim Brotherhood movement that was challenging his rule. This brutal retaliation was still fresh in Syrians' minds. But with the new generation in power, they hoped that Hafez al-Assad's son would loosen some of the restrictions that hampered everyday life. To the disappointment of people throughout Syria, the new president merely paid lip service to reform, and nothing much changed, and after Hama, few dared to challenge the authoritarian regime.

On Saturdays when Doaa was little, the old city market—or souk—would fill up with locals and visitors from across the border in Jordan, who came to buy high-quality produce at good prices, and to trade the tools and fruits of agriculture. Sitting on the main trade route to the Persian Gulf, Daraa attracted people from all over the region; people came together here or made a point of visiting as they passed through. At its heart, however, was a close-knit community of extended families and friendships that spanned generations.

Children in Daraa, as elsewhere in Syria, stayed with their families well into adulthood. Sons remained at home after marriage, bringing their wives into the family home to raise their children. Syrian households such as Doaa's were packed with family members, several generations under the same roof, sharing a single home. When a growing family overflowed out of the rooms on the first story of their dwelling, another floor would be added and the house would extend upward.

At Doaa's house, part of the ground floor belonged to her uncle Walid and aunt Ahlam and their four children. Next to him was Uncle Adnaan, with his family of six, and Doaa's grandfather Mohamed and grandmother Fawziyaa had their own room. On the upper level, Uncle Nabil had a small room with his wife, Hanadi, and their three boys and two girls. Doaa's family of eight shared the ground-floor room closest to the kitchen, the busiest and noisiest part of the house. All the main rooms were set around an open courtyard, typical of old Arab houses, where the children would dash in and out, coming together to play when school was out and between meals. The rooftop also offered space for the family to gather, and on hot summer nights, they would relax there until the early hours of the morning, the men smoking their water pipes, the women gossiping, all drinking sweet Syrian tea. On especially hot nights, the cool rooftop breeze would entice the family to roll out their mattresses and sleep under the stars.

The entire family—aunts, uncles, cousins—ate communal meals in the courtyard, seated on a carpet in a circle around steaming plates of food. At mealtimes, Doaa and her sisters ate ravenously, scooping up food with pieces of thin pita bread wrapped around their fingertips.

Doaa's father cherished these moments with his family, for it was the only time during the day that he could spend with his daughters. As soon as the meal was over, and he had finished off the last dregs of his sugary tea, he would pedal his bike back to his barbershop to work until midnight.

The love, conflicts, joys, and sorrows of living with a large clan affected every part of Doaa's daily life. And under the rooftop of this loving family, tensions were beginning to arise.

By the time Doaa was born, her parents already had three daughters and were facing pressure from the family to have a son. In traditional, patriarchal Syrian society, boys were more valued than girls as people believed they would support the family, whereas daughters would marry and turn their attention to their husbands and in-laws. Shokri, Doaa's father, was handsome, with curly dark hair. He had been a barber since the age of fourteen and had once worked abroad in Greece and Hungary. Shokri had had plans to return to Europe to find a job and a foreign wife, but after he met Hanaa, Doaa's mother, his plans changed. Hanaa was just finishing high school when they met at a neighbor's wedding. She was petite, had long, wavy dark hair, and striking green eyes. She and Shokri were instantly attracted to each other. She found him more worldly and self-confident than the other local guys, and she liked the way he dressed in bell-bottom jeans and played the oud, a string instrument that's considered the ancestor of the guitar.

Shokri and Hanaa were married when Hanaa was only seventeen. Their first few years together were peaceful and full of love, but slowly things changed. The first time Hanaa overheard her mother-in-law, Fawziyaa, complain that Hanaa and Shokri had no son was after Hanaa gave birth to her third daughter. Hanaa was shocked when she heard Shokri's relatives tell him that he should find himself a new wife to bear him a son. Despite having to fight against deeply ingrained prejudices and expectations, Shokri was proud of his growing daughters. However, his mother continued to criticize Hanaa and insisted that Shokri deserved sons. The family home, which had once been a sanctuary for Shokri and Hanaa, soon became a place of strife as some of Hanaa's sisters-in-law joined Shokri's mother in whispering and gossiping about her inability to bear sons.

When Doaa was born on July 9, 1995, Hanaa received the

usual halfhearted congratulations and murmurs of "Next time, *inshallah*"—God willing—"it might be a boy" from Shokri's family.

But when Hanaa looked at the solemn, earnest baby, she sensed something special about the little girl. When a well-respected and wealthy family friend visiting from out of town came by one day to see the new baby, she helped establish Doaa's place in her family. The friend, unable to have her own children, had an acute feel for the family dynamics and sensed the pressure Hanaa was under to have a boy and decided to help her. When the family gathered in the kitchen to welcome their special guest, she took Doaa carefully in her arms and held her gently. She looked down into the tiny baby's serious face, placed a finger on her forehead, and announced, "This one is special." Referring to the meaning of the name Doaa, the friend added, "She is truly a prayer from God." Before departing, the friend gave Hanaa ten thousand Syrian pounds—a small fortune—as a gift for Doaa. The rest of the family was astonished. The friend's exotic status as a wealthy resident of the Gulf States commanded respect. After that, Shokri's mother always insisted on holding Doaa, and for a time no more insults were hurled at Hanaa.

As Doaa grew up, she enchanted most everyone she met. She was extremely shy, unlike her more outgoing sisters, yet people always felt compelled to draw her out of her shell. She had a sweetness about her, and every time Hanaa took her out, people on the street commented on her beautiful chocolate-colored eyes framed with long eyelashes and her calm demeanor.

"From the start," Hanaa remembers, "we knew she would bring luck to the family."

Three years after Doaa was born, Hanaa gave birth to another daughter, Saja, and two years later to a sixth, Nawara. Suddenly the talk of "poor Shokri" with no sons flared up again. Also now, the eight members of the family were all living in a thirteen-by-sixteen-foot room with one window.

The rest of the extended family was growing as well, as Doaa's aunts and uncles also had more children. Large families are common in Syria, since the birth of a child is considered lucky, and a big family is a sign of a couple's happiness as well as assurance that they will be taken care of in old age.

Yet with close to thirty people living in one house, friction was beginning to grow among the women. It was impossible to cook for so many people at once, so the communal meals that had once brought everyone so much joy came to an end. Instead each family would have a turn in the kitchen. Hanaa had the first shift, so every day she had to rush to the market, peel and chop vegetables, and cook everything in time to serve lunch when Shokri took his midday break from the barbershop at three. It was the main meal for the family, and for Hanaa it was important that it be special. She had always taken pleasure and pride in preparing this meal, but now she found herself rushing and trying to avoid any conflict with her in-laws.

Doaa and her family now ate breakfast, lunch, and dinner in their small room atop a plastic tablecloth they spread over the center of the floor. That room had now become the center of their universe. It served as a bedroom, sitting room, and dining room, all family activity happened within those four walls.

As the girls grew up, it became harder to cram their lives into it. At night, Doaa and her sisters took out their mattresses and, one after the other, laid them across the floor into every possible space, like puzzle pieces. Doaa always chose the space under the window so she could stare up at the stars until her eyes shut. When they were all finally asleep, Shokri and Hanaa had to step over a sea of tangled arms and legs to get to their corner of the room.

For Hanaa, the atmosphere in the crowded house had become intolerable. All too often, her sisters-in-law critiqued her for not having any sons. One evening when she overheard them gossiping about her in the kitchen yet again, Hanaa decided that she had had enough of these insinuations, the squabbles over the kitchen, and the unending noise. That night, when Shokri returned home from work, Hanaa stood in the doorframe with her arms crossed over her chest and tears fighting to escape her eyes.

"Either you find us another house, or you find yourself another wife," she demanded. "We can't stay here any longer." She stepped closer to Shokri. "It's not just about me now either. Ayat is fifteen and Alaa is thirteen. They're teenagers! They're fed up with sharing a room with all of us. They need their privacy. I'll leave you and ask for a divorce if you don't find us a new place."

Shokri had noticed the growing tensions and the difficulties the family was having getting by in their small room. After sixteen years of marriage, he could also see that Hanaa meant what she was saying. Her tight lips and fierce scowl told him that she would make good on her threat to leave. He knew that he needed to find a better-paying job so they could move to a better home.

Doaa, by then six years old, was oblivious of the simmering tensions and had no idea that she was about to find out, for the first time in her life, that her world was not as safe as it seemed. To her, the big house was still a place of happy memories: of intense smells of simmering meat and aromatic spices; of laughter and endless games with the cousins in the courtyard surrounded by fragrant jasmine flowers; of warm nights out on the roof listening to the hum of the adults chattering and puffing on the *shisha* pipe.

Barbering was the only work Shokri knew, but he asked around to see whether his old yellow Peugeot could be used to transport goods back and forth across the Jordanian border. The "yellow submarine" was the family's only transportation and also the family joke. Rusty and dented, it tended to break down on weekend drives, but it was Shokri's pride and joy. Now, it was the family's one hope for moving out of their stifling, overcrowded home.

Shokri found a Jordanian businessman who offered to pay him to fill up his car with packages of locally produced Syrian cookies and take them to customers across the border in Jordan.

For the next two months, Shokri left home at dawn to drive to the factory in Daraa, where he would stuff the Peugeot with boxes of cookies and pastries. At times, he could barely see out the rearview mirror because the car was so full. If border traffic was light, he could make the trip in five hours and get home in time to have lunch with the family before his afternoon shift at the barbershop. Doaa and her sisters loved his new job; every time he came home, he would bring them treats from Jordan. They would wait by the door for the *kubz ishtiraak,* a type of thin pita bread that they couldn't get in Syria, and Barbi-brand potato chips, which the girls liked better than the kind they could get at home. He also brought them dresses and other more stylish clothes than any they'd had before.

Then one afternoon, Shokri didn't come home. Hours passed with no word from him. Hanaa and the girls worried; Shokri never stayed away longer than a few hours without letting them know first. Hanaa asked everyone in the family for help. She solicited neighbors and friends. Finally, after hours of frantic phone calls, Doaa's aunt Raja learned from a friend in Jordan that Shokri had been arrested. Border officials had discovered that his car was carrying more than the allowed 220 pounds of goods. On top of that, the documents the factory owner had given Shokri allowing him to transport goods over the border were forged. Shokri was now being held in prison in Jordan.

The family knew that the prison conditions could be terrible and were fraught with worry. They imagined him sleeping on the floor of a crowded cell, hungry and unable to wash or exercise. They couldn't afford a lawyer, so the family was uncertain about how they could navigate the complexity of the Jordanian justice system.

As the days passed, their concerns mounted. Not only were they worried about Shokri's well-being, they also couldn't afford to live without him. They barely scraped by on the money he brought home, and now they had no income. Hanaa's family stepped in, giving them food and whatever extra money they could. As a poor family, the Al Zamels had no connections to influential people in the government who might be able to help, and they didn't dare alert local officials to Shokri's imprisonment in Jordan, fearing that it could cause him further legal problems upon his return.

The family was not permitted to visit the prison or talk to him on the phone. So they received news of Shokri sporadically from contacts living in Jordan, but it was mostly confusing and only made them more anxious about his treatment. Doaa and her sisters cried every day, and at night, after the girls were asleep, Hanaa wept as well, wondering if her husband would ever come home.

The whole extended family came together to find a way to get him out. Four months after Shokri's arrest, a friend of his brother's named Adnaan paid a well-connected lawyer in Jordan ten thousand Syrian pounds (the equivalent of $500) to help Shokri. The lawyer was familiar with the Jordanian legal system and knew the prison officials and the judge who would need to be bribed if Shokri was to be released.

With the ten thousand pounds, the lawyer bought the purest

Syrian olive oil—worth two hundred pounds a kilogram—for the officers in charge of the case and the finest cuts of meat for the judge. He persuaded the judge that Shokri had been tricked by the factory owner and was just a simple man trying to support his family. The bribes worked and Shokri was finally released from prison.

Doaa and her family almost didn't recognize the thin, heavily bearded man who arrived at their doorstep late one night. Once they heard his familiar voice, the girls ran to him, screaming with delight and throwing their arms around him. After four months, Doaa had her father back, and she never wanted to let him go again.

Normal life resumed quickly after Shokri's release. He went back to his days at the barbershop, while Hanaa continued to cook the family meals. Together they continued to pursue their dream of having a home of their own. Eventually they found an affordable apartment in a cheaper section of Daraa, and they packed up the girls and moved.

Doaa's second home was a three-room apartment in the underdeveloped, conservative, and poor neighborhood of Tareq Al-Sad. It took Shokri and Hanaa months to find the dingy, dirty apartment, which was in ill repair. But here they didn't have to worry about upsetting aunts and uncles, and the children could run freely and be themselves. The girls quickly set out to help their parents clean up the rooms and make them cheerful. Doaa's sisters immediately took to their new home.

Doaa, however, had trouble adjusting. She hated change and she missed her cousins. She especially missed her old school. It had taken her a long time to open up around her teachers and classmates, and now she had to start all over again. At her new school she hung back shyly while her sisters made new friends. She often feigned illness so that she wouldn't have to attend class. But Doaa was the kind of child that attracted kindness from others, and over time she slowly made friends and began to enjoy her new environment.

In 2004, the family celebrated the birth of Doaa's little brother, Mohammad, nicknamed Hamudi. At last, the family had a son. The girls adored him and fought over who got to take care of him. Now that there was a boy in the family, Doaa's aunts and uncles invited them to move back into the family home, but Hanaa refused. They were now settled in their place and had put down roots in their new neighborhood.

But when Doaa turned fourteen, the news came that the owner of the apartment they had come to love needed it back, and the family had to move yet again. Doaa, who despised change, would have to uproot her life once more.

Finding a new home on Shokri's modest salary seemed an insurmountable challenge. More people were moving to Daraa to find work, and rents were rising. But after a three-month search, Doaa's family finally found a place beyond their expectations: a modest three-room apartment in the leafy El-Kashef neighborhood with a small light-filled kitchen and a roof lined with grapevines. Shokri and Hanaa had their own bedroom, and the girls slept in a room that doubled as a living room during the day. By then the eldest daughter, Ayat, had married and moved in with her in-laws.

Doaa, though, saw no promise in their new home, just the irretrievable loss of the friends she'd made in the old neighborhood and the people who understood her without having to try. Once again in a new environment, she was overcome with shyness.

She refused to speak in her new school and her grades fell. At first, she resisted any gestures of friendship. No matter how much her older sisters Asma and Alaa urged her to make friends, Doaa retreated, showing them that no one could force her to do anything she didn't want to do. Both her shyness and her ferocious stubbornness protected her, allowing her to control unfamiliar situations. It took Doaa a long time to trust people or to allow anyone to see who she really was.

But slowly over time, as in the other neighborhoods, Doaa's walls began to come down, and she eventually came out of her shell. Doaa made new friends and often went on walks with them through the neighborhood, and they visited one another's homes to study, gossip, and talk about boys. They frequently went up to Doaa's roof—her favorite place in her new home—to bask in the sun. At dusk, they would move inside to play Arabic pop music and dance in a circle, singing along with the words in unison.

While eventually Doaa became happy with her new neighborhood and friends, it became clear that the life of a traditional Syrian girl was not going to be enough for Doaa. Her childhood stubbornness grew into a resolve to make something of herself. Daraa was a traditional community, but Doaa knew from soap operas and the occasional movie that some women studied and worked, even in her own country. The Syrian state had officially declared itself in favor of women's equality, and tension was growing between two factions: those who believed that women should be housewives submissive to fathers and arranged husbands, and those who felt that women could pursue higher education, careers, and husbands of their own choosing. Doaa's favorite teacher was a woman who told her female students, "You must study hard to be the best of your generation. Think of your future, not just marriage." When Doaa heard this, she felt a stirring inside her to break people's assumptions about her and to live an independent life.

After the sixth grade, boys and girls no longer shared the same classrooms. Doaa and her friends would talk about boys; however, it was not culturally acceptable to talk *to* them. At fourteen, she and her friends were approaching the traditional age for marriage. The other girls would make bets about who would marry first. But when Doaa thought about her future and what it might hold, all she could think of was helping her family.

Her favorite place outside of school and her home was her father's barbershop. She wanted to show him how she could be a useful and efficient worker, even if she wasn't a boy. From the time she was eight, Doaa would go to Shokri's shop to help him whenever she could. As Shokri trimmed and cut, Doaa swept the hair that fell on the floor and always appeared right at the moment he finished a shave, holding open a clean, dry towel. When new customers arrived, Doaa would slip into the small kitchen at the back of the salon and emerge with a tray of hot tea, or small cups filled with bitter Arabic coffee.

On Thursdays after school, Shokri let Doaa shave him with the electric razor. He would laugh at her earnest face and call her "my professional" as she concentrated on her task. This nickname stirred an extreme sense of pride inside her and only made her more intent on one day earning money to support her father.

So when her sisters Asma and Alaa married at seventeen and eighteen, and her family began to tease her, "You're next in line!," Doaa immediately let them know that they should drop the subject and that she wasn't interested in getting married anytime soon. After their initial surprise, Doaa's parents accepted that she would take a different path from other girls and would at times dream that maybe she could be the first in their family to go to university. Hanaa always regretted that she never had that chance and loved the idea of one of her daughters achieving her own professional dreams.

Doaa surprised everyone when she announced that she wanted to be a policewoman. "A policewoman?" Hanaa said. "You should be a lawyer or a teacher!"

Shokri hated the idea as well. He despised the thought of her patrolling the streets, mingling with all levels of society, and confronting criminals. And on top of that, he didn't quite trust the police. Shokri was old-school and believed it was a man's role to protect society, particularly to protect women, not the other way around. But Doaa insisted, saying that she wanted to serve her country and to be the kind of person whom people turned to in times of trouble.

While Doaa's father disapproved, and her sisters made fun of her for dreaming of becoming a policewoman, Hanaa didn't tease Doaa at all. Instead she talked to her and tried to understand her daughter's motivations. Doaa confided that she felt trapped as a girl. Why couldn't she be independent and build her own life? Why did it always have to be linked to a man's?

Hanaa admitted to Doaa that even though she had fallen in love with Shokri, she regretted getting married at seventeen. Hanaa had been at the top of her class in school and excelled in her math and business courses. She had hoped to go on and study at the university, but back then, women had few options other than marrying and starting a family, but Hanaa thought perhaps Doaa could be different.

When Doaa was invited by her aunts on a trip to Damascus, the cosmopolitan capital city, Shokri allowed her to go, hoping that the trip might satisfy her urge for adventure. Instead, her visit only increased it. Doaa was transfixed by the bustling city. She imagined herself wandering the streets, visiting the beautiful Umayyad Mosque, negotiating in the bustling trade at the souk, and walking the paths of the sprawling university where she hoped to one day study. Damascus opened Doaa's eyes and set her mind on the idea of a different kind of future than the traditional one prescribed for her.

But those dreams would soon be torn from her. On December 19, 2010, after clearing the dinner plates, the family gathered as usual around the TV to scan the satellite channels for the news. Al Jazeera was leading with a breaking story from Tunisia about a young street vendor named Mohamed Bouazizi, who set fire to himself after the police confiscated his vegetable cart. A lack of economic opportunity in the country had reduced him to selling fruit and vegetables, and when that last bit of dignity was taken from him, he ended his life in a horrifying and public show of protest. It was the beginning of what was to become known as the Arab Spring. Everything in the region was about to change.

Including in Daraa. But not in the way that the people of Doaa's hometown had hoped.

TWO

The War Begins

It all started with some graffiti spray-painted on a wall by a group of schoolboys.

It was February of 2011, and for months the people of Daraa had watched as repressive regimes throughout the Middle East were challenged and brought down. In Tunisia, disenfranchised youths, identifying with Mohamed Bouazizi's despair and reacting to his self-immolation, set cars on fire and smashed shop windows in their frustration and desperation. In response, the hard-line Tunisian president, Zine El Abidine Ben Ali, who had been in power since 1987, promised his people more employment opportunities and freedom of the press and said that he would step down when his term ended in 2014. However, his announcements did little to assuage the public. Riots erupted all over the country demanding the president's immediate resignation. Ben Ali responded by declaring a state of emergency and by dissolving the government. His hold on the

country weakened and his ring of supporters in the army and
the government turned against him. On January 14, less than a
month after Mohamed Bouazizi took his own life, the president
resigned from office and fled to Saudi Arabia with his family.

For the first time ever in the Arab region, a popular protest
had succeeded in bringing down a dictator. In Syria, families
such as Doaa's watched in amazement. No one imagined that
they could ever defy the Syrian regime. Everyone disliked some
things about the government—the ongoing emergency law,
worsening economic conditions, a lack of freedom of speech—
but the people had all learned to live with them. Everyone felt
that nothing could be done. An all-seeing security apparatus
reached into every neighborhood and kept an eye on trouble-
makers. Activists in Damascus who had demanded reforms
after the death of former president Hafez al-Assad had landed
in prison, which had intimidated people from speaking ill of
the regime, much less making demands—until now. The uprising in Tunisia made it seem to ordinary Syrians that anything
was possible.

Doaa, now sixteen, and her sisters began to press their parents for details about what was happening in the region, wondering whether it could happen in Syria as well. Their father
tamped down their enthusiasm, afraid to encourage them.
Syria was different from Tunisia, he told them. Their government was stable. What happened in Tunisia was a onetime
thing. Or so he thought.

Then came Egypt, then Libya, and Yemen. In each country, protests followed a different script, but all of them called

for the same thing: freedom. One man's desperate act of protest had ignited flames of revolt across the Middle East. The Arab Spring was born, stirring hope in the discontented, especially the youth, and fear in those who ruled them. When the uprisings swept over Egypt, Syrians took particular notice. The two countries had merged for a brief three-year period in 1958 into the United Arab Republic. Syria had seceded from that union in 1961, but cultural ties remained strong. So when Egyptian president Hosni Mubarak was forced to step down on February 11, 2011, many disgruntled Syrians celebrated the victory of his toppling as if it were their own leader.

Doaa and her family watched the television reports in awe as the thousands of demonstrators in Tahrir Square in Cairo erupted into joyous celebrations. They cheered along to the chants of *"Allahu Akbar"* (God is great) and *"Misr hurr"* (Egypt is free) streaming from their TV screens.

Daraa had always been considered a reliable base of support for President Assad and his Ba'ath Party. But after the fall of Mubarak, in hushed discussions, citizens of Daraa started to talk about their own oppressive regime. Who would dare confront the Syrian government? they wondered. Assad was known for meeting dissent with crushing violence. Maybe ordinary people rising up against an all-powerful system could change things in other countries, but not in Syria, they felt sure.

A group of defiant young boys on the cusp of puberty would be the first dissidents to gain attention in Syria. On a quiet night in late February 2011, inspired by the rallying cries that had dominated the Arab Spring, they spray-painted graffiti on their school wall, *Ejak Al Door ya Duktur* (You're next, Doctor), alluding to Bashar al-Assad's training as an ophthalmologist. After they finished, the boys ran home laughing and joking, excited by what they saw as a harmless prank, a minor act of defiance. They knew the graffiti might anger the security forces, but they never imagined their small action would provoke a revolution of Syria's own and lead to a civil war that would divide and destroy the country.

The next morning, the headmaster of the school discovered the graffiti and called the police to investigate. One by one, fifteen boys were rounded up and taken off for interrogation to the local office of the Political Security Directorate, the arm of the Syrian intelligence apparatus that tightly monitors internal dissent. They were then transferred to one of the most feared intelligence detention centers in Damascus.

Doaa's family knew some of the boys and their relatives. Almost everybody did. In the close-knit city of Daraa, everyone was connected somehow, either through marriage or community. No one was sure which of those rounded up, if any, had actually sprayed the graffiti. Some boys were pressed to confess or implicate friends. Others were interrogated because their names had been scribbled on the school walls long before the graffiti was painted. No one could believe that these kids had been arrested for such a minor act.

About one week later, the families of the boys visited Atef Najib, a cousin of President Assad's and the head of the local Political Intelligence Branch, to appeal for their release. According to unconfirmed accounts that became legend, Najib told the parents that they should have taught their children better manners. He allegedly mocked the men, saying, "My advice to you is that you forget you ever had these children. Go back home and sleep with your wives and bring other children into the world, and if you can't do that, then bring your wives to us and we will do the job for you."

This was the final insult to the people of Daraa. On March 18, protesters took to the streets, demanding the release of the boys. This came three days after hundreds of people staged a rare protest in the old city of Damascus, calling for democratic reforms, an end to the emergency laws, and the release of all political prisoners. They chanted, "Peacefully, peacefully," as they marched to announce the nature of their movement. Six protesters were allegedly detained that day.

On March 18, in a coordinated action, people in Damascus, Homs, and Baniyas also took to the streets along with the people of Daraa to demand the release of Daraa's children while chanting, "God, Syria, freedom."

Doaa stood outside her home and watched as protesters marched by shouting, "End the emergency law," and demanding the release of political prisoners, including the boys of Daraa. She stood at the edge of the sidewalk, just outside her front door, as the protesters passed right in front of her, so close that she could have reached out and touched them. The energy and promise of the demonstration exhilarated her. Her whole life she had been told that the people of Syria would never defy their government and that she had to accept things as they were. But as she stood there watching the demonstrators file past her, for a moment she felt the urge to step off the sidewalk and join them, to be a part of what would be a new Syria. Suddenly, to her surprise, the police began to fire tear gas at the protesters and blast them with high-pressure water cannons from advancing big trucks. Her excitement turned to horror as protesters ran screaming in all directions or fell helpless to the ground. The street in front of her home had, in an instant, turned into the site of a confrontation. Horrified, she retreated to the safety of the house.

Later that day, outside the Al-Omari Mosque in the center of town, demonstrators gathered and staged a sit-in, declaring their Friday protest a Day of Dignity and demanding the release of the boys and the resignation of the governor of Daraa. This time, the security forces at the mosque did more than fire tear gas. They opened fire on the protesters, killing at least four people.

These were the first fatalities in a war that would go on to kill over 250,000 and force half the country from their homes— over 5 million Syrians becoming refugees abroad and almost 6.5 million displaced inside the country. Much of Daraa's population would eventually be driven from their homes, while schools, homes, and hospitals would be reduced to rubble.

Reports of the use of force against peaceful demonstrators in Daraa made international news, and the response from the global community was swift. At the United Nations in New

York, Secretary-General Ban Ki-moon issued a statement through his spokesperson stating that the use of lethal force against protesters was unacceptable and urging "the Syrian authorities to refrain from violence and to abide by their international commitments regarding human rights, which guarantee the freedom of opinion and expression, including the freedom of the press and the right to peaceful assembly."

The secretary-general said he believed that it was the "responsibility of the government in Syria to listen to the legitimate aspirations of the people and address them through inclusive political dialogue and genuine reforms, not repression."

The Syrian government, however, had a different version of events. According to Syria's state news agency, SANA, "Infiltrators took advantage of a gathering of citizens near the Omari mosque in the city of Daraa on Friday afternoon to provoke chaos through acts of violence, which resulted in damage to private and public property." SANA claimed that the infiltrators had set cars and shops on fire and attacked security forces.

Despite the government's violent reaction, demonstrations continued to spread across Syria, as furious citizens demanded reform. On Mother's Day in Syria, which falls on March 21, SANA ran a story that quoted a source in the Assad administration, stating that a committee had been formed to investigate the violent clashes in Daraa and that they had decided to release a number of "young men."

The boys from Daraa were given back their clothes and

backpacks and taken back to their home, released in the al-Saraya square to a crowd of thousands of cheering demonstrators. But the excitement soon turned to horror as it became clear that some of them, some as young as twelve, had been tortured. Their backs revealed gaping wounds left by electric cables that the guards had used as whips. The boys had cigarette burns on their faces, and some had fingernails missing. Word of the boys' condition fueled even greater anger. Even in a regime known for suppressing dissent, the torture of children was unthinkable. The boys of Daraa became icons of the budding revolution, and the protests grew.

The government hoped the release of the boys would quell the movement; they sent a senior envoy on behalf of the president's office to speak to crowds of protesters. He reminded the crowds that the president had set the young prisoners free and that he was aware of the protesters' demands. The envoy also said that the question of who had instigated the violence that erupted following the arrests was being investigated, but it was believed that the perpetrators were people impersonating security forces. He added that President Assad was sending personal representatives to the families of the dead protesters to offer his condolences.

These gestures satisfied no one, and as the protests raged on, the government accused demonstrators of ignoring these actions in an attempt to overthrow the state. Security forces started entering the city in large numbers. In state media newscasts, demonstrators were charged with being linked to terrorists. Blame was placed on "outlaws" such as President

Assad's estranged cousin Ribal Rifaat al-Assad, who was ex-
iled from Syria as a child and who became a vocal critic of
the government, or Abdul Haleem Khaddam, an opposition
ex–vice president who had turned on the government in
2005, defected to France, and called for regime change. Assad
also claimed that foreign elements were trying to destroy the
country.

That Mother's Day, Doaa's world was changed forever.
Every year, as a family tradition, she, her mother, sisters, and
little brother would visit their grandfather for lunch and visit
the cemetery to read the al-Fatiha, the first chapter of the
Quran, over her grandmother's grave, an important ritual for
Doaa. After reading the al-Fatiha, the children would hand out
ma'amoul cookies filled with dates, and single flowers from
their bouquet, to the other cemetery visitors, receiving similar
small gifts in return.

On that particular day Hanaa's instinct was to stay home.
Outside the door of their home, the street that was usually
bustling with passersby and shoppers was eerily silent. There
was talk of snipers, checkpoints, and clashes between demonstrators and government forces. To get to her father's house,
Hanaa and her children would have to venture into the city
center, where the clashes were at their fiercest. On top of all
this, Shokri was at work and could not accompany them until
much later in the day.

However, Doaa wouldn't hear of staying at home. She loved
visiting her grandfather's old house with its budding garden
where she would play with her younger cousins. At least thirty

of her family members were expected to be there, an occasion she did not want to miss.

"Mama," she insisted, "we go every year. We can't stop doing what we love."

Hanaa eventually gave in, knowing that if she didn't take her, Doaa would probably attempt to go on her own, leaving her at home worrying. Throughout the unrest in Syria, Hanaa wanted to give her daughters and Hamudi a sense of normalcy. However, nothing about the journey that awaited them would be normal.

Hanaa decided that the safest way to get to her father's was to go by taxi. Dressed in their best clothes, and carefully carrying boxes that held chocolate cake and assorted cookies, they set out.

At first, Hanaa's fears seemed unfounded. She walked out the door with Doaa, Saja, Nawara, and Hamudi and looked out to their street in El-Kashef. Fewer people than usual were out, but the shops were still serving customers and people were going about their business. Doaa spotted the usual gathering of neighbors in the shady square; the popular Abu Youssef falafel shop had its regular line of people waiting to order and the corner store where Doaa and her sisters bought sweets and chips had its door wide-open. For a moment the family forgot the violence that was sweeping through their city and upsetting the peace of their lives. Doaa strolled down the street smiling at the thought of visiting her grandmother's grave and spending a day with her family.

It was only a fifteen-minute ride to Doaa's grandfather's

house. Normally, taxis were abundant and cheap: thirty-five Syrian pounds for the ride to the city center. But that day, the few cars that drove by had their windows up and wouldn't slow to Hanaa's waving arm. Finally, a taxi stopped and the driver rolled down his window to tell them his price—250 pounds, a 600 percent markup. He said this was his "risk fee." Doaa was appalled that the driver would charge so much, but if they wanted to get to her grandfather's, they had no choice but to pay the driver's price.

They piled into the taxi, careful to not crush the cake or wrinkle their good clothes. Doaa caught sight of herself in the side mirror and smoothed her brightly patterned veil, wanting to look her best for the celebration.

The young driver was extremely nervous, breathing hard and constantly looking over his shoulders. As they made their way through the militarized zones in Daraa, they heard gunshots, making the driver jerk in his seat and Doaa think that perhaps her mother's fears were not unfounded. At every turn, they were stopped at a military roadblock. The driver tried to get around them by taking back roads and promised to take the family as close as he could to their destination.

As they neared the city center, Doaa spotted dark gray smoke rising a block away. They turned a corner and saw a police station on fire. Flames bloomed over its roof and shot violently out of its windows, and the smell of smoke began to fill the taxi, burning Doaa's throat. Police officers ran from the building to escape the flames, and the driver slammed on the brakes. "The protesters set it on fire," he shouted as the car screeched to a halt. But Doaa could barely hear him over the roaring of the fire and the shouts of people on the street. Scanning the scene through the windshield, she suddenly saw through the smoke protesters throwing rocks and shouting at the fleeing police. She pressed against the window, trying to get a clear view of what was happening.

"All hell is going to break loose now." The fear in the driver's voice terrified Doaa. "I'm sorry, but you have to get out. Keep close to the walls or they will shoot you." Doaa couldn't believe what she was hearing. This driver was going to leave them in the middle of this chaos? And why would her own government shoot her just for being on the street? Reluctantly, Hanaa paid the driver and the family got out. Hanaa kept Hamudi close, while the girls clustered together. The heat from the fire pressed against them as they began to walk as fast as they could away from it, looking around warily. Doaa's heart raced as she realized that her mother had been right. Things were unraveling. The demonstrators they saw were no longer carrying olive branches and throwing stones, now they were setting fires, and the security forces were fighting back with water cannons, tear gas, and live artillery, and Doaa's family was right in the middle of it. She was the one who had insisted they go. She was the reason her family was in danger.

With the crackling sound of gunfire erupting nearby, Hanaa grabbed Hamudi's hand and they all ran, heads down, to the closest building. Feeling exposed, they pressed against the wall as bullets ricocheted above their heads. They couldn't see where the bullets were coming from and weren't sure how to avoid them. Doaa's mind couldn't process that people were shooting at her. Part of her couldn't believe what was happening around her, how her quiet, normal life had so turned in an instant that her family were now huddled together in fear as bullets flew through the air and fires raged through the street. Another part of her was coolly thinking up a plan for how to protect her family. She knew that they had to keep moving. Going back home was just as dangerous as going forward, so they decided to press on toward their grandfather's house. At one point they dropped to their hands and knees and crawled through the streets. "Keep close to the wall!" Doaa called to her siblings ahead of her. Hamudi and Nawara started crying. Doaa ignored the sour taste of fear in her mouth as she tried to comfort them: "Don't be afraid. Get up now and run!" She knew that if they panicked, they were more likely to be killed. The family ditched the cake, stood up, and moved carefully along the walls, retreating to alleyways before moving farther up the road again. A walk that should have taken ten minutes took them an hour.

Finally, they reached the house in the Abassiya neighborhood and frantically banged on the door. Doaa's uncle opened it and pulled them into the house, his face pale with worry at the sight of his family in the midst of the gunfire. "Are you crazy?" he shouted at Hanaa when they were all safely inside. "Didn't you know what it's like outside?"

Saja, Nawara, and Hamudi were in shock. They quickly retreated to the back of the house, away from the sounds of shelling and death, trembling in fear. Doaa, however, felt that she had to know what was happening. Minutes after she greeted her relatives, she dropped a bag of cookies on the table and ran up the stairs to the roof, knowing that from there she would have a view of the square where they'd seen the clashes. Hanaa shouted after her not to go, but Doaa ignored her.

She pounded the rest of the way up the steps, shoved open the door, and ran to the chest-high wall surrounding the roof's edge. Breathing hard, she peered over the wall to the square in front of her grandfather's house. Throughout her childhood, Doaa had spent hours on that roof, watching the quiet plaza surrounded by shops and homes. She scanned the neighborhood now, transfixed by the protesters who had amassed on the square and were chanting, "We want freedom," as they marched with signs and olive branches toward a line of black-clad security men. Unlike the protests a few blocks away, this demonstration in the square across from her grandfather's home was peaceful.

The protesters were a mere five hundred meters from Doaa's position. She had the perfect vantage point to watch the demonstration unfold. Protesters stood in lines and were walking slowly forward across the square when security forces began firing tear gas at them. The metal canisters flew through the air, striking some protesters before falling to the ground and spewing gas. Some people fled, while others continued marching and chanting, "No to the emergency law" and "The Syrian people won't be humiliated." Many dropped to their knees, rubbing their stinging eyes as the tear gas choked their breathing. Then, to Doaa's horror, she saw officers raising their rifles and shooting live ammunition directly into the crowd. She heard herself shout, "Dear God," before a wave of tear gas reached her mouth and seared her throat. The chemicals burned her eyes, and she started coughing uncontrollably. She began to feel faint as she gripped the edge of the roof's wall and watched people fall to the ground, some wounded, some not moving at all. Even from a distance, Doaa was certain that they were dead, and she began sobbing at the brutality of their deaths. The government she had grown up wanting to serve as a policewoman was now shooting its own people, the people from her grandfather's neighborhood. She realized that everything she'd grown up believing about her country was wrong.

"Get down here!" Doaa could hear her mother's panicked shouts from the top of the stairs. Half-blinded by smoke and tears, Doaa ran back to the stairway. The moment she reached the bottom of the stairs, she collapsed into her mother's arms, gasping from the tear gas and trembling in shock. It was the first time Doaa had seen someone die in front of her, and she hated that she could do nothing about it. She was a powerless bystander.

Eyes watering, Doaa and her mother felt their way down the stairs and into the house. They retreated into a bedroom to recover and to try to make sense of what Doaa had seen. After some minutes, her grandfather coaxed her out. He wanted to maintain the rituals of their Mother's Day meal, and the family began eating in a hushed and heavy silence. But when Doaa drew the fork to her mouth, queasiness overtook her and she left her plate, filled with her favorite foods, untouched. Shokri burst through the door just as they were about to eat dessert. He joined them for coffee and sweets, but announced that they would be leaving before dark. Although the shooting was over and the protesters had retreated, the atmosphere outside was tense. "We can visit grandmother's grave another day." This time, Doaa didn't argue.

When they left the house, huddled close together, they saw bloodstains on the pavement where the shooting took place. The streets were deserted, save for a few men who were carrying the wounded into cars to take them away. Everyone's eyes started to burn and water from the tear gas that lingered invisibly in the air. Shokri led the family to a busy adjacent street that seemed unaffected by the uprising and violence that had taken place only a block away, and hailed a cab to take his family home.

Later they found out that demonstrators had also set fire to the Ba'ath Party headquarters and to a courthouse. Two branches of Syriatel, the phone company owned by the billionaire cousin of President Assad, Rami Makhlouf, had been targeted as well. Fifteen demonstrators were killed that day, according to eyewitness accounts, and scores injured. The government in Damascus, hoping to contain further unrest, announced that it would investigate the deaths but immediately began placing blame on local officials in Daraa. After that, the protests only grew in size, and more clashes occurred between demonstrators and the police. Meanwhile, the death toll mounted. In reaction to the government's brutality, a wing of armed opposition began to emerge from the peaceful protest movement.

Soon after the Mother's Day incident, Hanaa joined her sister on a visit to a friend of theirs, the mother of fourteen-year-old Ahmad, one of the boys who had been arrested. When Hanaa returned home, she was shaken and tearful. Ahmad was thin and gaunt, a ghost of his former self. "We almost didn't recognize him when he came home," his mother had told Hanaa. When she'd met with the boy, he had sat motionless, staring into space, unable to answer when they spoke to him. His swollen face was covered with red, shiny wounds, and his arms were blotched with bruises. Not only that, his knuckles were cut open and his fingernails were missing. His mother explained that his hands had been beaten with cables as punishment for the graffiti.

As word of the boys' mistreatment and abuse while in prison spread and the death toll of protesters continued to climb, more and more people joined the weekly protests at the mosque and demonstrators began to add to their original demands of ending corruption and the emergency law. They were now calling for regime change. The protests were growing quickly in size and frequency, and more soldiers started pouring in from Damascus to subdue the movement.

Doaa heard that women were being encouraged to take part in the demonstrations. After what she'd seen on her grandfather's roof, and hearing about Ahmad's bruised and beaten body from her mother, she was eager to join in. Something in her had shifted. The shy girl who had once feared change now felt driven to be a part of a revolution.

One of the demonstrations took place in her neighborhood, and many people from the countryside and surrounding areas came to participate. The atmosphere was jubilant. The people of Daraa started to believe that they could make a real difference in their country. When Doaa heard the shouts of the demonstrators approaching her home, she rounded up her sisters, her brother, Hamudi, and her friends Amal and Hoda and joined a row of women and other young girls in the back of the crowd. Doaa was exhilarated. For the first time in her life, she felt a sense of larger purpose, and she was determined to play a part in what she hoped would be a movement for peaceful change in the country she loved.

The more demonstrations she attended, the bolder Doaa grew, and she found different ways to contribute to the cause. One of her roles at a protest was to help people who had been exposed to tear gas by squeezing lemon onto a cloth that they could place over irritated eyes, and by cutting onions in half to provoke tears that would wash away the chemicals. One of her most dangerous tasks was to pick up tear gas canisters and throw them back at the security forces. The hot canisters burned her hands and she risked a face full of tear gas if the canister went off while she was holding it. She also ran the risk of attracting the attention of the security forces, but she didn't care; she was now wholly committed to the revolution, and her friends were beginning to get involved as well.

The protests eventually became social events where young

people would gather to share their hopes for the future. Amal and Hoda would often join Doaa and her sisters after school and on weekends at protests, whenever their mothers allowed it. But most of Doaa's friends were confined to their homes and would wait anxiously for her to tell them what had happened at each gathering. Doaa's conversations with her friends were no longer about boys, marriage, or neighborhood gossip. Now they talked only about resistance and rebellion.

At night Doaa no longer watched TV, but rather spent her free time thinking up inspiring rally cries and slogans to print on signs that she would bring to demonstrations for others to carry. She also began making bracelets and rings out of beads that were the colors of the revolutionary flag: red, black, and green. Each took her several hours to make, and when she ran out of beads, she had to beg her father to buy her more. Shokri refused at first, worried that Doaa was risking her safety making the revolutionary-themed jewelry, but in the end, as almost always, he gave in to her. Doaa wore the bracelets on both wrists and gave them out to friends, telling them to hide the jewelry under their sleeves when security forces made their rounds. She knew it was risky to be caught with such jewelry, but she was determined to contribute to the cause in any way she could. Her mother was paranoid that someone might find out that Doaa was making these little symbols of rebellion and feared that Doaa might be arrested, so Hanaa took to hiding Doaa's materials when she was out, but Doaa would eventually find them again and would go back to work on her jewelry at night while her parents slept.

"I'll go mad otherwise," she explained to her parents. She couldn't demonstrate at night, when only men were protesting, but she couldn't bear to sit by and do nothing.

The protests were so close to her house that she could hear the chanting as the demonstrators marched by. Each time she heard them, Doaa felt compelled to join in. During the day, she would throw on her jeans and a sweater and drape the flag of the revolution over her shoulders, preparing to go out. Watching her dress, her mother would implore her to stay home, out of harm's way.

"*Hayati* [my life]," Hanaa would plead, "please don't go. The security forces will recognize you and take revenge."

But Doaa wouldn't listen. "Mama, we can't sit at home and do nothing."

Hanaa knew that she would be in for a battle if she tried to stop Doaa from going out, and deep down she was proud of her daughter's courage and determination to be part of the revolution that could change Syria, so she let her go.

With the passing days, Hanaa noticed a transformation in Doaa. Instead of being shy and fearful and always resistant to change, Doaa now embraced it. Her enthusiasm would fill the air as she recounted stories about where she had marched that day and what had happened along the way.

Shokri would listen to Doaa's stories with dread. He was terrified for his daughters. He had heard stories circulating of women being stripped and raped by security men in front of their families. Others had simply disappeared. This was his worst nightmare, and he felt choked with worry as he left for work each day, leaving the girls and Hanaa alone.

When Shokri was home, he insisted that the girls stay inside at all times except to go to school. But Doaa fought his instructions. "*Baba*, you tell us that we have to stand up for our rights, and yet you won't let us go out and join the demonstrations," she complained.

Shokri shook his head. "It's my job to protect you and your sisters. Leave the demonstrations to the men of this city." He began insisting that Hanaa keep everyone home while he was off at work. But Doaa was defiant. She cried and sulked, refusing to eat or speak for days. She felt useless stuck inside the house.

Several times when Doaa was feeling particularly restless, she snuck out to join a demonstration. Shokri was furious when he discovered that she was missing, but he could do little. Eventually he gave up on trying to keep her in the house away from danger. Doaa's stubborn will simply outmatched his own.

The protests became part of daily life in the neighborhood. Men, women, and children came together to participate or watch. Doaa often bumped into cousins and school friends, and whenever she saw her closest friends, Amal and another friend who was also named Doaa, she would grab their hands and they would sing, chant, and march together in unison.

On March 30, 2011, President Assad gave a speech to parliament, addressing for the first time the unrest swallowing his country. As he walked into the chamber, members of parliament stood, enthusiastically clapping and chanting in a loud chorus, "God, Syria, and Bashar." As Doaa watched the coverage of the speech that night on the evening news, she held out hope that he was about to give in to the protesters' demands. Instead, while he admitted the deaths in Daraa had happened, he referred to them as isolated cases and a "mistake." Every citizen, he noted, has complaints, and his government was working to resolve them. But now, he warned, "conspirators" were at work pushing an "Israeli agenda" that was influencing those who had taken to the streets in good faith. He called those behind this conspiracy "foreign agents," labeled the demonstrators "terrorists," and claimed that the Arab satellite television channels were part of the scheme that was "creating chaos under the pretext of reform." He did announce that he might consider some changes to the system, but only after the country had returned to stability and the economy had improved. He claimed that the videos and photos the media were broadcasting to their audiences—showing government forces subduing civilians— were fake, and he pledged that he would not give in to the demands of those he considered terrorists. The prime minister, looking on, chanted, "God, Syria, and Bashar," in agreement.

Doaa was confused as she watched the broadcast. When Assad was talking about "terrorists," was he referring to her friends, family, and neighbors? *We are not terrorists!* she thought adamantly. But when it came to the shooting of unarmed demonstrators in Daraa, all Assad would say was that "mistakes" had been made and that "not all the demonstrators were conspirators." He wouldn't condemn the acts of brutal repression that were carried out by the security forces. At that moment Doaa realized that the struggle was just beginning and her country was coming apart.

After the parliament speech, unrest continued to spread across Syria, with protests erupting in the cities of Damascus, Homs, Aleppo, Douma, and Latakia. For a time, it seemed as if the tide was turning in favor of the opposition, as people throughout Syria turned against the government. Emboldened, the protesters vowed they would keep marching until their demands were met. Then, to their surprise, on April 21, just two months after the graffiti incident, President Assad announced on state TV that he would abolish the emergency law that had been in place since 1963.

For the opposition movement, this concession was too little and too late. The abolition of the law was no longer enough; people now had their sights set on regime change. But they soon realized that President Assad was working on a transformation of his own—to fortify his power by replacing the old system he'd inherited from his father with a new one under the pretense of fighting terrorism. Assad changed the laws so that anyone whose actions could be seen as damaging to the status of the nation or insulting to the ruling party or its leaders, or anyone who participated in demonstrations or bore arms, could now be charged with aiding and abetting "terrorists."

In response to these announcements, the protests swelled. The following day, in what became known as the Great Friday, demonstrations took place simultaneously in over twenty cities and towns across the country. Once again, security forces used tear gas and live ammunition to subdue protesters.

On the streets of Daraa, the standoffs between protesters and government soldiers were becoming increasingly violent, but this didn't deter Doaa, who went out anyway. One evening, just as a protest that Doaa, Nawara, Ayat, and Saja had taken part in was winding down, security forces suddenly appeared and advanced on the crowd with their guns raised. Everyone knew what would happen next—tear gas and beatings, possibly even death. People panicked and began screaming and running in different directions. Doaa lost track of her sisters in the mêlée. But as people scattered in all directions, Doaa could hear someone yelling after her—one of the organizers.

"Hide the loudspeaker and the *tabla* [drum]," he shouted, shoving them in her direction. "If they catch us with them, they'll arrest us!" Anyone caught with protest paraphernalia would be associated with the demonstration and could therefore be classified either as aiding terrorists or terrorists themselves.

Without hesitation, Doaa grabbed the drum and loudspeaker and shoved them under her *abaya*. These days, Shokri demanded that if the girls insisted on going out in the streets, they had to wear an *abaya*, a long black garment that covered them from head to foot. Women wearing them attracted less attention and it also allowed them to blend in with other women in the street, offering a layer of protection to Doaa and her sisters. At first, Doaa resisted—she hated the hot,

A

HOPE

MORE

POWERFUL

THAN

THE SEA

ONE

A Childhood in Syria

The second time Doaa nearly drowned, she was adrift in the center of a hostile sea that had just swallowed the man she loved. She was so cold she couldn't feel her feet, and so thirsty her tongue had swollen in her mouth. She was so overcome with grief that if not for the two tiny baby girls in her arms, barely alive, she would have let the sea consume her. No land was in sight. Just debris from the shipwreck, a few other survivors praying for rescue, and dozens of bloated, floating corpses.

Thirteen years earlier, a small lake, rather than the vast ocean, had almost taken her, and that time Doaa's family was there to save her. She was six years old and the only one in her family who'd refused to learn to swim. She was terrified of the water; just the sight of it filled her with dread.

During outings to the lake near their home, Doaa would sit alone and watch as her sisters and cousins splashed and dove and somersaulted into the lake, cooling off from the sweltering Syrian summer heat. When they tried to coax Doaa into the water, she steadfastly refused, feeling a sense of power in her resistance. Even as a small child, she was stubborn. "No one can ever tell Doaa what to do," her mother told everyone with a mix of pride and exasperation.

Then, one afternoon, Doaa's teenage cousin decided that she was being silly and that it was past time for her to learn how to swim. As Doaa sat obliviously drawing shapes in the dirt with her fingers and watching the others splash around, he crept up behind her, grabbed her by the waist, and lifted her up as she kicked and screamed. Ignoring her cries, he swung her up over his shoulder and carried her to the lake. Her face was pressed into his upper back while her legs dangled just below his chest. She kicked hard against his rib cage and dug her fingernails into his head. The children laughed as Doaa's cousin stretched out his arms and released her into the murky water. Doaa panicked as she smacked facedown into the lake. She was submerged only up to her chest, but she was paralyzed with fear and unable to position her legs to find footing. Rather than floating to the top, Doaa submerged, gasping for air but instead gulping water.

A pair of arms pulled her out of the lake just in time, lifting her to the shore and into the comforting lap of her frightened mother. Doaa coughed up all the liquid she'd ingested, sobbing, and vowed, then and there, to never go near the water again.

Back then, she had nothing else in her world to fear. Not when family was always around to protect her.

shapeless garment that hid her identity. However, on that night she was grateful for the cover. Cloaking the drum and loudspeaker under the *abaya* could allow her to get them to a safe location. Her home was just two streets away, so she turned and ran in its direction.

After she'd taken only a few steps, two cars screeched to a stop in front of her. One was filled with protesters, the other with security forces pursuing them. As the policemen jumped out of the car to arrest the protesters, Doaa realized that she was in trouble. If they caught her with the *tabla* and the loudspeaker, she'd be arrested as well or maybe worse. Struggling to keep panic at bay, she frantically looked around her and spotted an abandoned, partly constructed building just behind her and ran for it. The security forces, intent on capturing the protesters, didn't notice her. So with heart pounding, Doaa ran to an empty room on the second floor and hid behind a pillar. There she waited silently, trying to catch her breath. But a few moments later, the building was crawling with police looking for demonstrators. Doaa held her breath, afraid to move. Her mouth was dry, her chest was tight, and her arms shook as her grip on the loudspeaker and the *tabla* weakened. If they fell to the ground, she would surely be caught. Doaa began to pray under her breath for strength.

After agonizing minutes, she heard the sounds of the police making their way out of the building, back out to what was left of the demonstration. Breathing a sigh of relief, she set the drum and the loudspeaker down to give her aching arms a rest. From inside the building she watched as the police searched nearby shops and restaurants for people to arrest. Finally, when she couldn't see any more officers outside, Doaa picked up the drum and the loudspeaker and sprinted out onto the street to make her way home. The moment her feet hit the pavement, she realized she'd made a mistake. One of the security men had not left the area and was standing just outside the building, only a hundred meters from where she had been hiding. He immediately spotted her dashing from the building.

"Get her!" he shouted, pointing at Doaa. "She's one of the protesters!"

Terrified, Doaa ran as fast as she could. Not only was she still hiding the *tabla* and the loudspeaker, but the independence flag was also draped around her shoulders. There was no way she wouldn't be arrested if she was caught. Doaa quickly rounded a corner and was momentarily out of sight of the police. She pounded on the first door she saw.

"Let me in," she pleaded through the crack in the door, "Please hide me or they'll arrest me!"

When the door opened, it felt as if God himself had heard her plea. A woman about the same age as her mother embraced her and quickly pulled her inside, closing the door to sounds of gunfire. She rushed Doaa to the back of the house.

"Change your clothes now. Here, take my daughter's *abaya* and put on a different veil. If they come, I'll say you're my daughter."

But Doaa refused to take the woman's clothes. She didn't

plan to stay long and also didn't want to put the woman in further danger. Instead Doaa sat huddled in the corner of the room, alone and shaking, until the sound of bullets outside died down. Every few minutes, the woman came in to check on her: "Stay here until nightfall, *binti* [my daughter], then it will be safe to go home. We can hide your things for another day."

When darkness fell an hour later, Doaa thanked the woman for saving her life. Knowing she had to return home, Doaa tentatively opened the front door and stepped outside. Security officers still roamed the streets but, having shed the independence flag, Doaa didn't looked suspicious in her *abaya*. All the officers saw was an ordinary Syrian girl walking with her head bent modestly down. Doaa's home was mere steps from her hiding place, and now so close to safety, Doaa walked as quickly as she could without attracting attention. She saw her oldest sister, Ayat, standing outside.

"Doaa," Ayat screamed from a distance, "where have you been? We've been worried sick about you!"

Security officers turned toward them, and Doaa saw them looking at her with sudden interest. Terrified that they might recognize her, she ran for her house. The moment she reached Ayat, Doaa grabbed her sister's arm.

"Shut up, will you?" she hissed as she looked over her shoulder. "You're drawing their attention." The men were now staring at the girls and pointing. Doaa and Ayat continued toward the house, and as soon as they reached the door, Hanaa pulled them both inside, hugging Doaa close to her. She had been overcome with worry when the other girls had come home without Doaa and was terrified that she'd been arrested.

As her family gathered around her, Doaa recounted what had happened. Her siblings were impressed by her bravery, and Hanaa was too relieved to be angry.

"*Habibti* [my love]," Hanaa said, holding Doaa close and stroking her hair, "I know you are brave, but you are still a girl, and God knows what they'll do to you if they catch you. You must be careful."

Doaa turned toward her father, expecting him to embrace her in the same way her mother had. But instead, he stood with his fists clenched and his face red with fury. Doaa took a step toward him, then stopped, recognizing the anger in his body language. Shokri's temper didn't show itself often, but when it did, it was fearsome. She had never before seen such anger in his eyes. Doaa knew that this time she'd gone too far.

"I forbid you from ever going to another demonstration again," he thundered.

Saja and Nawara shrank away from him while watching Doaa apprehensively. Hanaa tried to calm his temper, while Doaa began to cry in frustration. She couldn't bear the thought of staying away from the protests. But Shokri was adamant. He was terrified of what might have happened had Doaa been arrested. There were rumors that girls had been raped in the streets in front of their parents for stepping out of line and disobeying the law. Other women were arrested and never heard from again. Shokri decided that he would lock Doaa in the house if that's what it took to keep her out of the streets and prevent her from endangering herself. For the first time in Doaa's life, he turned his back on her tears. "That's my final word," he stated resolutely.

Despite her stubbornness, deep down Doaa was still a traditional Syrian girl and knew when she had to obey her father. She knew she couldn't get around it this time, so she reluctantly agreed to stay indoors, but her acquiescence wouldn't last; her heart remained with the revolution.

THREE

The Siege of Daraa

Monday, April 25, 2011, started out like any other bright spring day. Doaa was on her way up to the roof to hang the family laundry, the one household task she didn't mind since she could do it while chatting with her best friend, Amal, whose balcony overlooked Doaa's roof. It was also a chance for her to see the comings and goings in the neighborhood from a prime viewing spot.

That morning she pushed open the door to the roof with one hip while balancing a plastic basket full of freshly washed dresses, scarves, and shirts on the other. The sun was warm on her face and a cool breeze ruffled her veil. As she shifted the heavy basket for a better grip, she heard a low, rumbling sound. Startled, she set down her load and rushed to peer over the edge of the wall. From four stories up, she had a clear view of the streets of El-Kashef—the bakery across the street, the sidewalks where the neighborhood children played. But now, instead of a familiar quiet, she saw people running in all directions, panicked and afraid. In the distance, she could make out large black shapes advancing toward the city. To get a better view, she leaned farther over the roof wall. As the shapes came into focus, she recognized that military tanks were slowly rolling down the street toward her house. The weight of the massive vehicles seemed to crush the surface of the street, and she could feel the roof trembling beneath her feet. Alongside the tanks she saw hundreds of armed soldiers marching, while military helicopters circled above, their loud propellers drowning out the usual sounds of the city.

Doaa gripped the roof wall tightly, feeling the rough concrete bite into her hands. A sense of dread sickened her as she remembered the stories she had heard about the city of Hama and what had happened there three decades earlier. President Hafez al-Assad had crushed the uprising then by ordering his troops to besiege the city. It's estimated that ten thousand to forty thousand people were killed during the takeover. The Hama massacre served as a cautionary tale in Syria, and emergency law was reinforced to quell dissent.

Watching with dread as tanks entered her city, Doaa couldn't help but wonder if President Bashar al-Assad would follow in the footsteps of his father and slaughter anyone who dared to challenge his authority.

While Doaa was pressed against the rooftop wall watching the tanks rumble into the city, her father was at work in the barbershop and her mother was out visiting family. Hamudi and the girls were outside playing on the street in front of the house, as Doaa's oldest sister, Ayat, who was visiting with her two children, looked on. They were all directly in the path of the approaching tanks and armed men.

Doaa sprinted across the rooftop and down the stairs two at a time. She burst out the front door to warn her siblings. "Get inside, for God's sake," she screamed. "You'll all be killed!" She grabbed Hamudi by the arm and pulled him into the house as her sisters followed her inside. Angry and confused, Ayat snatched up her two little boys and charged inside after them.

"Have you gone crazy?" Ayat shouted. "What's come over you? What's happening?"

Doaa pulled Ayat to the front window that looked out onto the street. "This is what is happening!" Doaa pointed. "They're going to wipe us out!"

As the tanks neared the house, they looked even more menacing. Doaa could see the silhouettes of men dressed in black with balaclavas wrapped around their faces hiding their identities, standing aloft in the gunners' hatches. It seemed as if they were pointing their guns directly at Doaa's house and family.

Overcome with fear, Doaa ran to the phone to call her mother but got no response. Desperate, she pressed the redial button over and over, but the phone only rang and rang. Her father didn't own a cell phone, and the barbershop had no phone either. So instead, Doaa continually dialed her mother, staring intently at the phone, as if by doing so she could make her pick up.

As the soldiers marched through the town, panicked

thoughts began to flood Doaa's head as Ayat's children began to cry. *Where are my parents? Are they safe? What if they don't come home?* Doaa wondered in fear. Huddled together inside the back room that was farthest from the street, Doaa and her siblings clung to each other. Doaa hated feeling helpless, but she could do nothing to protect her family from the threat outside the door.

After what seemed like ages, their mother suddenly burst through the door. Though she had been only minutes away, it had taken her over an hour in a taxi to get through the checkpoints and back to the house. She looked exhausted, and worry filled her eyes as they darted from Ayat and the grandchildren to Hamudi, then to Doaa, Saja, and Nawara, assuring herself that everyone was safe. Hamudi ran to her and she knelt and gathered him into her chest as the rest of the girls swarmed around them, throwing their arms around their mother. "It looks like doomsday outside. Where's Shokri?" Hanaa asked breathlessly, scanning the room and noticing her husband's absence.

The family dreaded the worst. What if Shokri had been picked up in the ensuing chaos outside and was thrown in jail? For hours the family waited, peering through the front window, trying to see as far down the street as they could. Doaa tried to convince herself that her father was just delayed at checkpoints as her mother had been, but worry nagged at her. Finally, the girls glimpsed him through the window, hunched over and hurriedly pushing his bike toward the house. His usually immaculate clothes were rumpled and his dark hair was damp with sweat. Hanaa rushed to open the door for him. Once inside, he looked around the room just as Hanaa had done, counting everyone inside, relieved to see his entire family safe. The family gathered around him as he told them about the soldiers he had seen around town in key positions, prepared to attack at a moment's notice. He glanced at Ayat and her children. "It's too dangerous for you to go home. You'll have to stay the night."

As the sky darkened outside, Doaa went to switch on a lamp to brighten the room, but nothing happened. She tried two more lamps before realizing that the electricity had been cut off. Hanaa then went to the kitchen to make some tea, but only a few drops of water dripped from the spout; running water had also been shut off. Confused, she returned to the living room and gathered Hamudi into her lap as Doaa, Saja, and Nawara stared out the windows. They watched apprehensively as the soldiers outside seemed to settle in for a long stay, leaning against the tanks parked right outside the door. The family slowly began to realize that this situation could be more permanent than they had anticipated.

Shokri turned on their battery-operated radio and tuned in the news to learn more.

Daraa is under siege, the broadcaster announced. *The army has been sent to root out the terrorists who are trying to destroy the country.*

A cloud settled over the family as this news sank in and they began to wonder how this would affect their daily lives.

Later that night as the rest of the family went to sleep, Doaa lay awake, unable to ignore the feeling that something terrible was about to happen. She lay as still as she could and listened to the sounds of Saja and Nawara breathing deeply next to her, as the laughter and shouts of the soldiers echoed outside. Finally, she drifted off to sleep, only to be awakened at 4:30 a.m. by the alarm she had set to wake her for morning prayers. She reached out toward the clock, and just as her fingers pressed down on the button to shut off the alarm, the few lights that had been on when the electricity was cut flickered back on. The electricity must have been turned on again just at that moment when her alarm rang. Disoriented, Doaa sat on her bed for a moment, trying to gather her wits about her, then suddenly she heard screams and the rattle of gunfire in the street. Jolted alert by these disturbing sounds, Doaa dashed to the front window to find people running in the streets and the tanks moving. Ayat joined her at the window, and soon the whole family was gathered around, watching in terror as the security forces began to smash into people's houses. Men and boys as young as eleven were being rounded up in the street and forced to put their arms behind their backs and to walk with their heads bowed. The soldiers shoved them into cars, shouting at them that they were terrorists.

Shaken by what they saw, Doaa's family decided to turn to the Quran for comfort. They forced themselves away from the windows and gathered in the living room, trying to read their morning prayers together, as it dawned on them all that the siege would not end soon.

Later that morning, Hanaa began to plan how the family

would get by on what she had in the kitchen—some leftover bits of cheese, yogurt, and salad in the refrigerator, along with a few things she kept in the cupboard: jam, pickles, olives, and some canned vegetables. She found a bag of rice, but remembered that there was no water to cook it with. On top of that, Ayat and her children still couldn't go home, so the little food they did have would have to stretch to feed three more people. After taking stock, Hanaa quickly decided that the family would have to make do with only one small midday meal until they were able to leave the house again to gather more food.

At each meal, Hanaa did her best to portion out what little food they had as they all took tiny sips of water from one glass that they shared among the entire family, drawn from the remaining stock of bottled water that they had in the house. Disconnected from their TV programs during evening power cuts, they sat together by candlelight, taking turns reading the Quran. They often started with the Ayat al Kursi verse, which asked God to protect them through the night.

Once all their candles had been burned, they sat in the darkness, listening in huddled silence to the sounds of gunfire, explosions, and screams outside. Sometimes, they even heard the ricocheting pangs of bullets as they hit the walls of their house. Every night they went to bed hungry and wondering how long their confinement would last.

One week passed with their only contact with the outside world being when armed men in uniform and muddy boots banged and kicked at their door, demanding to be let in to search the house. This disturbing and intrusive ritual was performed as often as three times a day. Each time Shokri rose to let them in, he was cooperative and obedient in order to protect the family. Sometimes, the soldiers entered the home and pointed their guns at them, one member at a time. "We're looking for terrorists," they would state. *That means me,* Doaa thought as she realized anyone who'd taken part in a demonstration was now being classified as a terrorist by the state. She was certain that they knew that she and her sisters had been out demonstrating and were trying to scare them into confessing.

One time one soldier looked directly at Doaa and said, "You want freedom, you dogs? We'll give you freedom." Then he and his men began sweeping things off the shelves, toppling over books and breaking vases and other trinkets. They then moved into the kitchen and knocked over the last bottle of precious olive oil along with the remaining jars of preserved fruits and vegetables, smashing everything onto the floor. The family was left to clean up the mess and fret over how they would survive with almost all their reserves gone.

Another time during a search, the visiting soldiers took Doaa's mobile phone and scanned through it for photos or videos that might implicate her in the demonstrations. She had been warned that taking photos of the demonstrations could associate her with them, so she had wisely refrained from documenting her involvement.

One soldier even pointed his gun at Hamudi, who was only six at the time. Trembling in fear, he clung to his mother. Hanaa was terrified that the soldiers might arrest him as they had other young boys. She shielded him in her arms and prayed the soldiers would leave them alone. When they finally left the home, Hanaa was flooded with relief. But every time the family's house was searched, the fear that someone would be taken away was renewed.

One day, as Doaa was closing the door behind a group of soldiers who were just leaving the house after searching the property, another group suddenly pushed open the door again, demanding entry. One of the soldiers shoved his rifle into her stomach and pushed her to the floor.

"Why are you closing the door in our faces?" he barked at Doaa, keeping the gun pressed against her stomach.

Doaa lay there frozen still. "Your colleagues were already here," she said, looking up at him. "They just finished conducting a search."

After a few seconds, he lowered his weapon and turned his attention to Shokri. "Take me up to your roof," he demanded. He insisted the family go up the stairs ahead of him and the other soldiers so that if rebels were upstairs waiting to ambush, the family would be shot first. Shokri led the way with the rest of the family crowding into the stairway behind him. As she glared over her mother's shoulder at the soldiers, Doaa felt her rage swell. *This was her home, her family. What right did they have to order them around and threaten them?* She despised seeing her proud father forced to obey these bullies, and she bit the insides of her cheeks to stop herself from hurling insults at them. The soldiers quickly discovered that there was nothing on the roof, and Doaa breathed a sigh of relief as this second group of soldiers left the house. The family had survived yet another raid.

Each time a search was conducted, Shokri feared that the soldiers might kidnap the girls. So he made Doaa and her sisters sleep in their *abaya*s so that they would be fully covered in case of a raid in the middle of the night, which was starting to become routine. He also gave each of his daughters a knife for protection. "Stab any man who comes too close," he advised, and instructed them to keep the knives hidden under their *abaya*s during searches.

The night after her father had given them their knives, Doaa gathered her sisters and created a pact. "If any soldier tries to rape us," she whispered so her parents couldn't hear, "we must be ready to kill ourselves. We cannot live with that shame. Our honor is all we have left." Thirteen-year-old Saja and ten-year-old Nawara took her hands and nodded grimly in agreement.

Not long after that, soldiers came to the house to inspect the back room where Doaa and the family were sitting. One of them was in his early twenties with long, unruly black hair. He ogled Doaa in a way that she found inappropriate. She shifted uncomfortably under his gaze. Though Shokri had instructed them all to stay silent during the searches and not to antagonize anyone, this time Doaa couldn't contain herself. She glared back at him, not bothering to hide the loathing and anger behind her gaze.

"Why are you staring at me like that?" the soldier demanded.

"I'm a free person," she replied defiantly, her face livid with anger. "I can do whatever I want." Doaa knew the word *free* would set the soldier off.

Annoyed, he charged toward her demanding to see her identification.

"I don't have one," she admitted.

"Don't have one? Why not? How old are you?"

"Fifteen."

"So why don't you have an ID yet?"

"I tried to get one. I applied for an ID at the government registry, but they refused to issue one to me."

The soldier laughed when he heard this. "Then why don't you go to a demonstration for *that*?"

Doaa saw clearly that her participation in the demonstrations was no secret. She felt her heart thump inside her chest as this dawned on her, but she refused to show her fear. "Yes, maybe I will," she replied flippantly.

The soldier's eyes flashed with anger as he lifted his gun in warning. "Don't talk back," he ordered.

The whole family froze in fear, waiting for the soldier's anger to explode, but after glaring at Doaa for some time, he finally lowered his gun, turned, and walked toward the door, muttering as he left, "You'd better watch yourself because, don't forget, we're watching you."

When the door slammed behind him, Hanaa was furious. "Never speak to the soldiers like that! You're putting yourself in danger!"

"You're putting all of us in danger!" Shokri fumed as he

rose to stand over Doaa. "From now on, you remain silent whenever they enter," he demanded.

Doaa was too shaken and angry to answer. She didn't even bother to nod in acknowledgment. Instead, she just lowered her head and stared mutinously at the floor. Deep down she was glad she had defied the soldier, but she also knew that she could never admit this to her family. She did feel proud when later that day her sisters whispered to her that they respected her courage, while at the same time expressing their wonder at what had become of their shy sister.

On the morning of May 5, eleven days after the siege began, Hanaa stood in front of the empty cupboard, now desperately worried about how she would feed the family. All of a sudden she heard an amplified voice blaring outside the window. Too afraid to open it since that was against the rules of the siege, the family pressed as close to the window as they could to make out the announcement from the police car driving through the neighborhood: "Today, there is a curfew. From 7:00 a.m. to 1:00 p.m. you must remain in your homes. From 1:00 to 2:00 p.m. women have permission to leave their houses to shop for food. All women leaving their homes will be searched. The curfew will resume at 2:00." The siege had been lifted, if only for a brief moment.

Hanaa breathed a sigh of relief, thinking only of the groceries she would finally be able to bring home to her hungry family. But Shokri was outraged by the announcement. Touching women was considered unacceptable in Islam. He felt that this order to search women was an attempt to provoke the men of Daraa in the government's desperation to control the population.

"I will never let them lay a hand on you, as long as I live," Shokri said incredulously, refusing to let Hanaa leave. But she was adamant; the children were growing thinner by the day and Ayat's young children were constantly crying from hunger.

"We have to feed our family. There's nothing left in the house." Hanaa pleaded gently, meeting her husband's eyes. "If I have to suffer the indignity of being searched, I will."

Shokri looked around at his frail family and reluctantly agreed.

When Hanaa finally stepped outside her home, she found that the neighborhood was completely occupied by soldiers, tanks, and weapons. Just a few hundred meters from the house, she saw a group of more than one hundred officers sitting around long tables laden with food. She realized that while her family and the other citizens of Daraa had starved, the soldiers had been feasting just outside their doors.

Hanaa tentatively began to cross the street toward the bakery. But before she'd taken more than a few steps, she could feel the weight of the soldiers' eyes watching her. It suddenly seemed as if every soldier on the street were staring at her. Panicked at the idea of being searched, Hanaa couldn't move forward. Trembling in the street, she quickly decided to return to the safety of her house and hurried back inside.

Moments later, there was a knock at the door. Shokri answered it, tentatively cracking the door open.

"Who is the woman who just left this house?" a man's voice asked through the opening. "I want to speak to her."

Shokri summoned Hanaa, who came to the door and found a tall, stern-looking army general standing there with his machine gun strapped to his side.

"It was me, General. I wanted to get bread for my family."

"So why did you suddenly turn back?"

"I was too scared, General." Hanaa kept her eyes lowered respectfully. "There were too many men in the street."

As he listened to her, the general's eyes showed a glimmer of sympathy and his voice softened. "I insist that you get food for your family. But you need to go now, while there aren't any snipers. They're never out between noon and four."

Hanaa and Shokri were stunned that this man seemed to be helping them. "Thank you, General, thank you. *Allah ma'ak* [God be with you]," Hanaa replied, collecting her shopping bag and following him outside. He returned to his group of soldiers, but watched as Hanaa disappeared into the store, then later emerged with her allotted six loaves of bread. When she passed him on her way back to the house, he asked gently, "Did anyone bother you?" She shook her head, keeping her eyes lowered. "Good," he said. "You should get home now."

Hanaa quickly made her way home. Back in the kitchen, she remarked, "There is humanity left in people," as she unpacked the bread and the family gathered for a simple feast.

As the siege wore on, Doaa's family slowly discovered that many young soldiers were not out to hurt them. Four soldiers in particular—dark, handsome Ali; green-eyed Bahaar; short,

boyish Nero, and tall Abdul Aziz—who were all stationed outside their house, were always kind to the family. Ali was nicest
of all, often slipping Hanaa a loaf of bread and a few tomatoes with a shy smile while on duty. House searches conducted
by these young men were performed halfheartedly, as they usually moved through the rooms quickly and left the shelves untouched and the drawers unopened. Sometimes they lingered
inside the house, charging their mobile phones, chatting about
the news of the day, or playing with Ayat's toddlers. On a
couple of occasions, they even gave Shokri money for food.
Doaa and her sisters felt strangely protected by them and didn't
grip their knives in the same way they did when other soldiers
entered their home. Doaa saw clearly that those kind, young
soldiers didn't want to be there any more than her family
wanted them there.

One day there was a desperate knocking on their door.
Prepared to face yet another raid, Doaa was surprised to find
a young man in his early twenties, shaking in fear. He was
carrying a gun and had his face covered with a kaffiyeh, a check-
ered black-and-white scarf.

"Help me!" he pleaded. "I'm with the FSA and the regime
is after me. The soldiers are going to kill me!" Doaa had heard
that many men who were part of the demonstrations had now
joined together to form an armed opposition to the government and named themselves the Free Syrian Army.

"Come inside," Doaa responded immediately, looking up
and down the street. While she couldn't leave him out there to
be killed, she also couldn't be caught sheltering an FSA sol-

dier. So she quickly came up with a plan to hide him. She and Saja took four cardboard boxes and got the young man to sit against a corner of a room that was crowded with mattresses and small tables. They arranged the boxes around him and covered them with a blanket to resemble a chair. It looked lumpy and a little awkward, but they thought it might work if the sympathetic soldiers conducted the next raid.

They waited an hour before the inevitable knock came. To their relief Ali was standing at the door, but just behind him they saw an officer they didn't recognize, and they began to panic.

The soldiers filed in, and after a quick look around the room Ali announced, "There's no one here." Doaa was certain he noticed the new "chair," but he said nothing about it. She held her breath waiting for the soldiers to leave. But then the unknown officer asked Ali to lead him to the roof. They marched upstairs as the family waited below. After several minutes they returned, satisfied with their search. They finally left the house, and when the door closed behind them, Doaa and Saja yanked off the blankets and deconstructed the chair. The young man pulled himself up from his crouched position. Hanaa brought him a glass of water, and as he reached for it, he kissed her hand, looking around at the family. "Thank you. You saved my life!" After some hasty good-byes, he mounted the stairs to the roof and escaped over the side of the building.

As Doaa watched him go, a sense of triumph and satisfaction filled her chest. After weeks of bowing down to soldiers and feeling helpless, she had won a small victory against the men occupying her home. She began to wonder what else she might be able to do.

During the eleven days of the siege and since the start of the uprising, the state-run news agency, SANA, announced that the government had completed its mission to "chase out elements of terrorist groups" and to "restore security, peace, and stability" to Daraa. General Riad Haddad, director of the military's political division, announced that the army would withdraw its six thousand troops in phases and that the city would return to normal. But during those eleven days, while Doaa and her family had remained locked inside their home, the world had taken notice of their plight, and news reports began to release details of the more than two hundred deaths and one thousand arrests that had occurred during the siege. According to the Syrian state media, as many as eighty soldiers had also died. As the news spread around the world, US secretary of state Hillary Clinton warned the government of Syria that there would be "consequences for this brutal crackdown," and European leaders began to discuss sanctions. Human rights groups reported that at least six hundred people had died across Syria in the seven weeks since the crackdown on demonstrators had begun, and eight thousand had been jailed or gone missing.

Doaa noticed with relief that the tanks outside their house began to leave their positions, and fewer armed soldiers patrolled the streets. Despite all this, it became clear that things were far from back to normal. Decomposing bodies of protesters lay uncollected in the streets, and the stench of rotting flesh filled the air. On top of the death, there was destruction. The girls had not gone to school since the siege began, and they were anxious to get back to see their friends and resume their studies. But the school remained shut, and the road they once took to get to school was now lined with pockmarked buildings, some of them abandoned, with doors left open revealing the intimate spaces where lives had once been lived.

Still, Shokri was determined to get back to work as his money had run out during the siege. But every day when he left for his shop, his family wondered if he would make it back home alive. They heard stories of cruel government snipers who seemed to make a game of shooting people, regardless of age or gender. As people came out of their homes to collect the bodies of the dead left in the streets, those people were shot at as well. No one was safe under all this madness, and Hanaa urged Shokri to be cautious, reminding him that she herself had witnessed a man shot dead as he was leaving the mosque. They had also seen a video of a pregnant woman lying dead in the street having been shot in the belly.

Scared but determined to support his family, day after day Shokri made his way through the checkpoints on his bike and opened his shop. But most of his clients were too afraid to come. His salon was in the heart of the al-Saraya neighborhood, the operations center of the regime in the old town, which had become a target for the now well-armed opposition. Sitting in his shop, he watched the battles between government forces and the opposition unfold around the courthouse and other government buildings.

"There's a war going on in this city and you expect people to get their hair cut? Are you crazy?" his neighbors would ask him. But Shokri was sure that some of his customers would come for their ritual shave and trim, and he desperately needed their business to feed his family. "My death will come when God decrees it," he would tell people.

One afternoon in late June, as he was cutting a client's hair, Shokri heard gunfire. He left his client's side to peer out the door and saw a group of men running from the shots.

"There they go again," Shokri told his client, and went back to trimming his hair. By then, Shokri had grown accustomed to the sound, and he took pride in continuing his work in spite of the unrest around him.

"Another day in the revolution," replied his client wearily. "But I still need a haircut, it's been months. God damn them all."

Suddenly, both men heard a loud rumbling noise. In the reflection in the shop mirror, they could see a huge vehicle approaching slowly, straight toward the salon. It looked as if it were about to roll right over them. The client jumped out of the chair, gasping in fear, and pulled the towel from around his neck, dropping it to the floor.

"I haven't finished your haircut," Shokri pleaded, trying to calm him. But the client disappeared around the corner, his hair only half-cut. The tank then suddenly turned and rumbled around the center of the square.

Doaa, meanwhile, was learning how to gauge the mood of

the city by the number of bullet casings she found on the street in front of her house each morning. She longed to join the demonstrations that had resumed after the siege, but they were smaller now, and no longer peaceful. The air of celebration was gone, replaced with anger and desperation. She knew her father would never allow her to return.

After most of the tanks and the soldiers left the city, a new threat emerged as bombings began. On summer evenings, the family sat outside their house in a strange new ritual and watched other neighborhoods in the city light up as missiles fell. They counted how long it took for the bombs to land and guessed what kind of destruction had occurred from the clouds that mushroomed above. The sounds of heavy artillery shelling and explosions replaced birdsong.

"*Alhamdullilah* [thank God], it didn't land here," they said to each other, feeling guilty at the way war had hardened them. Sometimes they would witness the Free Syrian Army firing a rocket-propelled grenade, and they would all cheer, hoping that it hit its target.

Nowadays, the only thing Doaa and her sisters were allowed to do was cross the street to buy food from the supermarket or bread from the bakery. But prices had almost doubled and any better-quality food was even more expensive.

One day, the family had run out of bread, so Doaa, Saja, and Nawara went out to try to buy some. As they walked toward the bakery, soldiers called out to them, "Where are you going? Go back!"

Doaa answered, "We are only going to get bread." But the soldiers kept insisting that they should return home. The girls stopped in the middle of the street and bent their heads together, whispering, "Should we turn back around?" They were so hungry their stomachs ached. While they were scared to disobey the soldiers, they also couldn't bear the idea of going another day without any food. After a hurried discussion, they agreed to make it look as if they were going back home. They had heard that a Palestinian refugee camp in a neighborhood a thirty-minute walk away had food. They decided that they would go there instead. So they turned down the street in that direction. They were about two hundred meters from the camp when the soldiers spotted them again. Furious that the girls had defied them, the soldiers began shouting, "Go back, you dogs!"

This set Doaa off. They weren't protesting or threatening the soldiers; she and her sisters were just trying to keep their family from starving, and the soldiers were getting in the way of that and being nothing but bullies. Without turning around, she shouted over her shoulder, "We need to eat! You're starving us!"

"We just want to get food," Saja added.

Before the soldiers could respond, the girls heard shooting in their direction and the sound of a tank moving toward them. They weren't sure whether they had become the targets of army snipers for defying the soldiers' orders or if they were suddenly caught in a cross fire. They immediately threw themselves to the ground, landing hard on the asphalt. Doaa felt the air forced from her lungs as she pressed her face to the ground and heard bullets flying above them like angry bees. Nawara felt the stinging brush of a bullet grazing over her back. If it had been a quarter of an inch lower, it could have killed her.

As soon as the gunfire ceased, Doaa and Saja helped Nawara up and ran through the side streets into the camp, hiding in alleyways until they felt it was safe enough to return home. They gave up on getting food, as the fear of being shot overcame their hunger. As they approached their home, all three of them were pale and shaking, aware of how close they had come to being killed. Nawara had a burn mark on her shirt where the bullet had skimmed her. Ali was on patrol outside their house, and he and his fellow soldiers noticed immediately that the girls were upset. His handsome, kind face creased with concern, Ali asked what had happened. As Saja and Nawara rushed into the house to Hanaa's embrace, Doaa stopped to tell Ali that they weren't able to buy any food for the family because they had been shot at. She walked back to her house feeling like a failure for coming home without food. An hour later, Ali knocked at the door and handed Hanaa a loaf of bread and a plastic bag full of ripe tomatoes. Grateful, Hanaa accepted his gift and quickly returned inside to make a meal for her family and to comfort her shaken daughters.

Now that the siege had been lifted and the protests continued, Doaa began to spend a lot of time up on the roof to hear what was happening on the ground. If she couldn't attend the protests in person, this would have to do.

Doaa and her sisters would join in the chants of "Allahu

Akbar" (God is great) and then "How can you kill your own sons?" and "Freedom!" Shouting along from their rooftop was a way of participating. Doaa knew that they had to be careful to not be noticed, as being on the roof made them a target for any snipers surveying the crowds from above. Anytime a soldier looked in her direction, her heart pounded. But despite her fear, being on the roof where she could see and join in the chants made her feel connected to the opposition.

One day, as she was in her usual position leaning over the edge of the roof and chanting the slogans along with the protesters, a soldier spotted her from a nearby building where he was stationed to observe the crowd, occasionally firing shots into the streets.

"Get down, *irhabiya* [terrorist]," he shouted at her. When Doaa didn't move, he threatened, "Get inside or I'll shoot you."

That day Doaa felt emboldened by her fear, and she shouted back, "You're the terrorist, you're the one killing people! I saw you!"

At this, the man raised his gun and pointed it directly at Doaa. She quickly realized, in horror, that this soldier really intended to shoot her, so she bolted for the door. As she did, she felt a gust of air as a bullet brushed past her ear and hit the iron door in front of her, leaving a dent before it ricocheted backward and dropped to the ground. Just an inch closer and she would have been dead.

She threw the door open and ran inside to the safety of her home. Catching her breath, Doaa was surprised to realize that despite the bullet's having just buzzed past her, she was not afraid. She wondered if she was becoming immune to fear. Every day they learned of more people that they knew who had been killed by government forces, but somehow, at this moment, she felt intuitively that the time had not yet come for her life to end. She felt that God had her destiny in his hands, and that the best way to serve him was to do what she believed was right and to follow the direction she received from her prayers. Doaa didn't want fear to conquer her or her family, and she was resolved to continue living this way.

Through the fall and long winter of violence and food, electricity, and water shortages, the Al Zamels, like all families, did what they could to get by in a city that had turned into a war zone. Shokri brought home just enough money to buy food, and families and neighbors did what they could to help one another.

Then one day in June 2012, when Shokri arrived at his salon, he found that two missiles had hit the roof, turning the back of his shop into rubble. For over thirty years, Salon Al Fananeen had been his source of income and part of his identity, and now it lay in ruins.

He surveyed the damage, sweeping away shattered pieces of mirror and cleaning the debris from the mangled chairs. He dug out his scissors and brushes, meticulously cleaning off the dust, then placed them carefully back on the half-broken shelf. He pushed the pieces of rubble from the roof to the far reaches of the shop, moved the only undamaged chair to the front, and waited all day for a customer. No one came.

When he returned home that night, Doaa noticed a change

in him. His shoulders slumped and his face was blank. He somehow looked smaller than usual. "*Baba,* what's wrong? What happened?"

"The shop . . ." was all he could say. The family tried to comfort him, assuring him that they were relieved to have him home all day so that they wouldn't have to worry about his safety all the time, but he found no comfort in their words. The loss of his shop took his spirit away. He spent the rest of the day sitting in the same spot in the corner of the house, chain-smoking, and only speaking if someone asked him a question. Doaa sensed that his losing his livelihood was like his losing his manhood, and she desperately wanted to find a way to help him, but the only thing she could do was try to keep his spirits up. "It will be over soon, *Baba,* we must be patient."

Shokri's shop wasn't the only one that had been destroyed. Ayat's husband's popular baklava shop down the street was also demolished by a bomb. He had come late to work that day, just minutes after the missile fell. "God saved me," he told the family. Days later, another bomb demolished his car. "That was everything I had," he told Ayat, then revealed his plan to flee for Lebanon where his brother lived. His brother could help find him work and he could send money home for her and the kids. Ayat's husband had no interest in taking part in the armed struggle for either side. He just wanted to continue to make a living for his family, so instead he joined a growing group of Syrians paying bribes at checkpoints to make their way out of the country for neighboring Lebanon to wait out the war. Ayat and the children would follow him not long after by paying a smuggler to get them to the border, and telling the soldiers at checkpoints along the way that they were headed there to visit relatives.

More and more people began to leave Daraa, although the thought of fleeing home had never entered Doaa's mind. She was convinced that the uprising would soon end and that they could just start over and resume normal lives. She felt that the people who fled were abandoning a cause more important than staying alive, and she couldn't imagine ever leaving the home she loved so much.

However, as every day in Daraa became a lottery of life and death, the stresses of survival began to take their toll on the entire family. The girls suffered from insomnia and panic attacks, and they were always nervous and on edge, constantly bickering over small things. Hamudi would cry every time he heard a loud noise, and the sounds of the bombs outside made him hysterical. He clung to Hanaa's side, following her around the house, afraid to lose sight of her.

Doaa, too, was feeling the physical effects of stress. She lost her appetite and grew extremely thin. Hanaa suspected that Doaa was anemic. She also began to get regular sties in her eyes, and one morning she awoke to discover that her entire eyelid was completely swollen.

"We have to go to the doctor now, *hayati*," Hanaa said when she saw her. "Your whole eye is infected."

But a trip to the clinic was risky—they had to cross areas of fighting to get there, and it would take at least an hour. Despite the risk, Hanaa called for an appointment that day and found a taxi that would take them. Security forces were on every corner, and only a few civilians were on the streets. When Hanaa and Doaa arrived at the clinic, they hurried inside.

The doctor, a distant relative, took one look at Doaa's eye and said he would have to lance the sty immediately. With no money, Hanaa explained that they couldn't afford the five hundred Syrian pounds for the operation.

"Don't worry, my dear, I'll do it for free. We are family, after all," the doctor said, smiling at Doaa, "and I don't want you to lose that pretty eye." Doaa was too nervous about the procedure to smile back and held tight to her mother's hand.

When Doaa saw the long needle the doctor would use to inject anesthetic in her eye and the razor he would use on the sty, she burst into tears. The doctor comforted her, instructing her to close her eyes and pretend she was sleeping. Doaa obeyed and he quickly set to work. He injected the anesthetic in the sty and covered her eye with a bandage. Afterward he gave her a prescription for antibiotics and sent Doaa and her mother on their way with instructions to return in a week.

The operation hadn't taken more than an hour, but in that time, fighting had broken out in the streets. No taxis were to be found to take them home, and Doaa was beginning to feel dizzy after her operation. Hanaa's sister lived a fifteen-minute walk away, so Hanaa phoned to let her know they were coming, and they set off for her house. All Doaa wanted was to sit on the sidewalk and put her head in her arms. She felt weak and helpless and to walk had to lean heavily on her mother's shoulder while gripping her hand. As they walked, a car full of men who looked like government officials approached them and slowed down.

"Where are you going, sweetheart?" they called to Doaa, leaning out of the car. "What happened to your beautiful eye?"

Hanaa squeezed Doaa's hand tighter and whispered, "Don't respond, *habibti*. Keep looking down."

Doaa, her mouth dry with fear and still weak from the operation and the anesthetic, did as her mother ordered.

"Hey, speak to us when we talk to you," one of the men shouted. "It's rude not to reply."

Hanaa and Doaa remained silent, terrified that any acknowledgment would simply encourage the men. Doaa's aunt's house was now across the street as the men began to lose patience with the two women and started to get really angry.

"Hey, bitch," one of them shouted, "I told you, answer me when I talk to you." At this, the rest of the men began to laugh, clearly enjoying what had become a game to them.

Doaa looked around for help, but no one else was on the street. So they kept walking as the car trailed slowly behind them. They were steps away from Hanaa's sister's house when they heard the car door swing open behind them. The men were getting out of the car. Their game was over and they moved in closer to Doaa and her mother.

Hanaa and Doaa realized that they had to make a break for it. They ran toward the house. *"Ukhti* [sister]*!"* Hanaa cried out as she banged on the door, "Open up, someone's trying to kidnap Doaa!"

Within seconds, Doaa's aunt Iman opened the door and

pulled them inside. "I was praying to God you would make it," she told them as she slammed the door behind her.

Doaa was white with fear, and Hanaa worried that she might faint. Hanaa quickly guided her to the nearest chair as Iman rushed back to the window to check if the car was still there.

"You're safe, they're leaving," Iman told them.

"Rest now," Hanaa reassured Doaa, "the curfew is about to start. We're safe here."

"You don't know how lucky you are," Iman said. "Just yesterday I saw them take some girls to that park across the street. They're torturing people there! Every night I can hear screams coming from that place." Hearing this, Doaa's imagination went wild. If they had taken her, she would have used her knife to kill herself. She would never stand for the indignity of whatever those men had planned for her.

For now, Doaa was safe, although her ordeal wasn't over.

At nightfall, Hanaa and Doaa decided to head home. It was risky to be caught out after curfew, and—more urgently—they had to fill the prescription for antibiotics for Doaa's eye or else it could get reinfected. They decided to take a chance and walk the back roads to their home. Iman packed a small bag of food and gave Hanaa and Doaa five hundred pounds each. Cautiously, Hanaa and Doaa slipped out into the dark.

On their way back, they saw a small pharmacy with its light still on. Doaa stumbled inside after her mother, catching the pharmacist by surprise. She was shocked to see them at this hour: "It's dangerous to be on the streets now. What are you doing?"

"We need medicine. My daughter just had an operation," Hanaa told her.

Seeing Doaa's eye, the pharmacist quickly filled the prescription. Doaa was feeling dizzier by the minute. She wasn't sure she could keep standing as she fought back tears of anger and frustration.

The pharmacist handed them the medicine, saying urgently, "Go quickly. They just killed a man outside. I heard the shots, then I heard them throw his body in the Dumpster."

Terrified by this story, Hanaa pulled out some money to pay the pharmacist and prepared to leave immediately, but the pharmacist refused it. *"Allah ma'aku* [God be with you]," she said instead. "Walk with your heads down and don't look to your side where the Dumpster is."

But once outside, they couldn't help but look. Blood dripped from the bottom slot of the Dumpster onto the street. Doaa was sick with the realization of what had just happened, but they continued on. A little farther up the road, they heard the sound of a car approaching, so she and Hanaa quickly turned to hide in the shadows of the nearest building. There they waited and watched as a group of men got out of the car, opened the trunk, carried another body to the Dumpster, and threw it in. "Shoot him again to make sure he is dead," they overheard one of them say, then shots rang out through the air. The men piled back into the car and it disappeared up the road.

Doaa and her mother came out of the shadows to continue their journey home. "Mama," Doaa cried out suddenly, feeling nauseated, "I can't walk. I'm really going to faint."

Hanaa held on to her daughter. "*Hayati,* you must. We'll go slowly, I'll support you."

Summoning all of her strength, Doaa followed her mother. For the next hour, they crept along the walls trying to blend in with the buildings. When they eventually saw the lights of their house, Doaa thought she might faint with relief, while Hanaa said a prayer of thanks. They had never been more afraid than they were that day.

That night, while the children slept, Hanaa and Shokri decided it was time to leave Syria. It was naïve to believe that their lives would return to normal anytime soon, and they knew how close they had come to losing Doaa that day. Shokri had already lost his livelihood and worried it was only a matter of time before he would lose his girls. Their neighborhood was emptying day by day. All the men of fighting age had disappeared, having either joined the Free Syrian Army, been arrested, or been killed.

In the morning, Shokri picked up the phone and called the only person he knew who had the financial means and connections to help them—his son-in-law Islam, in Abu Dhabi. When he answered, Shokri told him, "We're leaving. Help us get to Egypt."

FOUR

Life as a Refugee

Doaa knelt on the backseat of the car. Through tears she stared out the rear window as her country faded away behind her. Saja, Nawara, and Hamudi were crammed in next to her, making it difficult for her to take a full breath. Her parents shared the front seat with Khaled, her father's friend who was driving them out of the country, staring steadily ahead. Out the window she could hear the muffled sounds of sporadic shooting, and her despair deepened as she realized that this would not be just a short family trip. Her sobs grew heavier as the reality that this departure might last forever began to sink in.

She did not want to leave. She'd promised herself that she would never abandon the revolution and had begged her father to let her stay behind. "Leaving Syria would be like taking my soul away from me," she told him, her voice trembling.

"I am your father and I need to keep your soul alive," he replied.

The night before they left, they had only a few hours' warning. They had to quickly bid good-bye to friends and had a wrenching farewell with Doaa's older sister Asma, who was staying behind with her husband and children. They also called Ayat, who had left several weeks before to join her husband in Lebanon. The call from Islam, the husband of Doaa's other sister Alaa, came at 10:00 p.m. He said that he was transferring money to them for ferry tickets from Jordan to Egypt and advised them to leave for Jordan at once. Doaa, Saja, and Nawara sobbed as they packed and hugged Asma and their cousins again and again. "You will be back," Asma assured them. *But when?* Doaa wondered, looking into her sister's face, trying to memorize it.

The next morning at nine, they packed their suitcases into Khaled's car trunk and piled into the car. At the last checkpoint on their way to the border, Doaa muttered aloud, "This feels like they are closing the lid of my coffin." She looked out the window and began whispering good-bye to everything she saw. "Good-bye, streets. Good-bye, trees. Good-bye, Daraa. Good-bye, weather. Good-bye." A tear dropped on the car seat as she leaned out the window for air.

Shokri twisted around in his seat to look at Doaa, his eyes filled with anguish as he took in her sorrow. He knew how distressed his family was, but he'd made the hard decision to leave behind the life they'd built together in order to protect them. He knew that Doaa and her siblings might not understand that now, but he wanted her to see that he was trying to do what was best.

"Do you think I wanted to leave Daraa?" he asked, fighting to keep his voice steady. He would have done anything to spare his family pain. "I don't have a choice. I won't risk you girls being kidnapped."

By that time, all three girls were sobbing. Khaled chimed in to offer his support to his friend: "Your father is right to take you away from this madness. He is only thinking of keeping you safe."

Doaa trusted Khaled, someone she had known all her life, and part of her knew that he was right. She was grateful to him for helping her father take care of the family and did her best to mask her disappointment. No one in the car could imagine it then, but months later they would learn that back in Daraa Khaled had been killed in the war.

There were seven checkpoints along the fifteen-kilometer route to the border. At one, security guards opened the trunk, then their suitcases, and tore through the family's belongings. At another, they were interrogated. The soldiers demanded to know why they were leaving Syria. "My husband is sick," Hanaa lied. "We have to leave to get medical care for him." A small part of Doaa secretly hoped they would be turned back so that they could go home again, but at her mother's response, the guard just shrugged and waved them on. When they finally reached the Jordanian border, Doaa looked over her shoulder at her homeland, taking everything in.

"I envy the mountains and the trees and the rocks because

they will be able to breathe Daraa's air and I won't," she whispered, taking one last, longing look at her home.

It was November 2012, one year and eight months since the violence in Syria first began. Though figures vary widely depending on who is counting, the Syrian Observatory for Human Rights, which tracks the death toll in the conflict, estimates that over forty-nine thousand people had been killed by that time. It was impossible to know how many had disappeared or were behind bars in government prisons. The war would only become more deadly, and by its fifth year, according to UN estimates, over 250,000 people would be killed and over 1 million injured. Meanwhile, 5 million Syrians, such as Doaa's family, would be forced to flee across borders, while 6.5 million would be internally displaced, often forced to move several times to other parts of the country where they could find pockets of safety. By 2016, Syrians would become the largest displaced population in the world.

As Khaled steered his vehicle to the Nasib border crossing, the family saw what must have been two hundred cars lined up for entry into Irbid, the border town in Jordan. They inched forward, watching as some cars ahead moved across the border while others were turned back. As they got closer to the front of the line, Doaa saw the tension growing in her mother's shoulders and the tightness in her father's jaw as he stiffened in the front seat. Doaa had been sitting still in the car for so long that she wanted to scream. Finally, when they reached the border control, the official told Shokri that crossing would cost ten thousand pounds per person. Shokri had only seven thousand

Syrian pounds and three hundred Egyptian pounds left to his name. He tried to negotiate with the border guards, but to no avail. The officers just folded their arms and shook their heads. Doaa wished she could shout in their indifferent faces. The family was ordered to turn around. Khaled suggested that they park the car off to the side for a moment to think up a new plan, and Shokri and Hanaa wearily agreed. They had left home that morning at nine, and with all the checkpoints and the lines of cars trying to leave, by that time it was almost midnight. They pulled the car over and stepped out, shivering in the cold November air and trying to formulate a new plan.

Doaa couldn't sit still another minute crammed in the backseat with her siblings. As soon as they pulled over, she climbed out of the car and stretched her arms over her head, her tight muscles aching after the long ride. As she walked around the parking area, she saw row after row of cars full of people trapped as she was. They were all refused entry to Jordan, but no one wanted to start their engines to turn back. Among the crowd she heard women crying and babies howling. Men and women wandered among the parked cars, asking for help and desperately trying to find some way to get across the border, while children sat on the ground too exhausted from the long journey to play. It looked as if half of Daraa were stuck at the border. Doaa surveyed the scene, wishing she could be anywhere but in this crowded, despair-filled parking area. Then all of a sudden, to her amazement, she spotted her uncle Walid, Hanaa's brother, sitting at a rickety table displaying a stack of newspapers. He was once an engineer, but had lost his job when the war started and had now resorted to selling newspapers at that very border crossing! For a moment, Doaa just stared at him, not believing that it was really him. Then, she rushed over. Intent on his reading, he didn't notice Doaa until she was standing right in front of him. Walid looked up from his paper, startled, then a smile of delight and recognition crept across his face at the sight of his niece. Doaa immediately began explaining what had happened, speaking as quickly as she could and pointing to the car. Walid's face grew more serious as he listened to her story, then he took both her hands in his and pulled her close to him. "Go back to the car and wait," he instructed her. "Don't go anywhere." Doaa rushed back to the car and told her parents what had happened, and they did as instructed. Within an hour, the Al Zamel family was on a list of people allowed into Jordan. They assumed that Walid had paid a bribe that set them on their way into exile as refugees.

Doaa and her family were lucky. Crossing the border was known to be fraught with danger and difficulty; it took bribes and several attempts to make it. As the war raged on, crossing would become much more arduous. Refugee numbers swelled in Syria's neighboring countries Jordan, Lebanon, and Turkey, as well as in Egypt and Iraq, and finding refuge would become increasingly difficult. Neighboring countries, concerned about security and wary of the numbers of refugees in their care, began to tightly control their borders, allowing only severe humanitarian cases to cross.

The Al Zamels were indeed lucky to leave when they did.

Crossing into Jordan, they headed to the border city of Irbid, where one of Shokri's brothers lived. He was there to pick them up as they arrived. They piled out of Khaled's car and said a grateful farewell to him, as he had to return to Daraa. The family spent the next three days in Irbid, waiting for their ferry to Egypt. Shokri was the most anxious of all of them to leave; after his time in prison, he was leery of spending any time in Jordan.

At daybreak on November 17, 2012, Doaa and her family boarded a bus for the coast. They traveled down the length of Jordan along the border with Israel, past the Dead Sea, and finally to the port town of Aqaba, where ferries departed for Egypt.

Nervously they waited to board. Doaa shifted from foot to foot in the long line to get through customs. Hamudi clutched his mother's arm, while Saja and Nawara sat on their suitcases, standing only to shuffle forward whenever the line moved. It felt as if every part of the journey were about waiting. Jordanian customs officials seemed to be singling out Syrians for security searches, and Doaa's family was asked to come forward with their luggage, while a group of Egyptian travelers were waved through. Doaa lifted her suitcase onto the table in front of the customs officers. When they unzipped her luggage, she looked at what she had hastily selected in the overwhelmingly emotional last hours at home: two dresses, a couple of pairs of pants, two blazers, a few skirts, several veils, and a few accessories. She stared at the meager contents of her suitcase and thought of the books she had left behind because they were too heavy—one about dream interpretation, a few novels, poetry by Nizar Qabbani, and a workbook on English grammar. She pictured her small teddy bear that lit up and made a kissing sound when she squeezed it, and her fashion sketches of the clothes she dreamed of wearing in a future she no longer had.

She suddenly looked away from the open suitcase, blinking to keep herself from crying. She mourned silently to herself, *I left my life back in Syria!* Not wanting to burden her family with more of her sorrow, she remembered that her treasured belongings were now being stored at her grandfather's house. She hoped that their presence there might protect her hometown and keep it safe for her while she was gone. If she left a part of herself in Daraa, surely she would someday return, she thought hopefully.

The ferry was delayed four hours by bad weather. Doaa sat waiting for the weather to change and dreading the next five-hour leg of her journey, which would take them across the Gulf of Aqaba. She had never overcome her fear of water and had never been on a boat. The waves were high, and they slapped against the sides of the vessel, making it rock back and forth at the dock. Though the ferry's large size and stable appearance gave her some reassurance that they would have a safe journey, she was still frightened. Every time a wave pushed the ferry against the wooden dock, Doaa jumped a little at the harsh scraping sound it made. She had to call on all of her stubbornness and courage to force herself to step aboard the ship once the time came.

As her mother and Hamudi settled with all their bags on the lower level, Doaa and her sisters rushed to the top deck for the fresh air. But while Saja and Nawara moved to the side of the boat to look at the sea, Doaa stayed as far from the edge as possible. For the first hour of the trip, her sisters leaned excitedly over the railing taking in the view, while Doaa sat unmoving at the center of the deck, gripping the sides of the bench she sat on for balance as the shores of Jordan faded from sight. When her fingers cramped, she shifted her weight, but didn't dare let go.

Saja turned back to look for Doaa. When she saw her face, she grew concerned. "Doaa, your face is sheer white!"

"It's just that I can't see the land anymore," she explained, looking toward the shore she could no longer see, trying to be brave. Even though she couldn't swim, the sight of land calmed her as she thought that she could make her way back to shore somehow if need be. As they drifted farther out to sea, Doaa finally admitted to her sisters, "I'm scared." She asked them to help her down to join their mother and Hamudi on the lower deck. Saja and Nawara obliged and the family clustered together down below, sharing a small picnic.

Finally, they reached the port of Nuweiba on the Sinai Peninsula. When the Al Zamels stepped off the ferry into Egypt, Doaa was so exhausted that she felt as if she could sleep for a week. Smiling officials greeted them as they checked their passports without much scrutiny, stamped the documents, and explained that they had an automatic six-month residency, which could be renewed. Mohamed Morsi was president at the time, and his government had an open-door policy for all refugees arriving from Syria.

The family waited in the immigration line, watching as other passengers had their luggage weighed, and noticed that many of them were getting charged for excess baggage. Shokri looked uneasily at his own family's luggage, worried that they would have to pay a fee, too, considering all they had brought with them. Doaa noticed the concern on his face and wished she had some way to comfort him. She knew they didn't have enough money to pay any fees. The family hesitantly approached the customs agents.

"We are Syrians seeking safety in Egypt," Shokri told them. "This is all we have left." Hanaa stepped up beside him, as Doaa and her siblings watched from behind for the customs officials' reaction. Doaa held her breath, waiting for another insult from an apathetic official.

To her surprise, the official manning the customs scale smiled at them and told them they wouldn't have to pay anything, even though their bags exceeded the allowed weight. "You are coming from war and suffering," he told them. "Syria and Egypt are bound together like family." Another customs worker came and helped them carry their luggage to the bus bound for Cairo and wished them luck, while a family who were standing at the shore watching people file onto the bus called out in their direction, "Welcome, beautiful Syrian people!"

Saja whispered that she felt like a queen. For the first time in months, Doaa felt both safe and welcome. They had heard that Egypt would happily take them in as refugees, and here, finally, was the proof. Yet despite the warm greetings, Doaa was still anxious about having to start over again, this time in a strange new country. Her instincts told her that tough times were ahead. She looked around the bus, taking in her new surroundings, and stopped when she noticed the look on her brother's face. For the first time in a long time, little Hamudi was smiling.

It took ten hours by bus on a bumpy desert road to reach Cairo. From there, they had to travel another five hours to the northern city of Damietta on the Mediterranean coast, where Doaa's brother-in-law Islam had found a home for them in the district of Gamasa. Islam's friend Abou Amad had arrived as a refugee a year before them, and they took a taxi from Cairo to his home. After offering them a simple meal, Abou led them to an apartment nearby that he had arranged for them to stay in. The flat, on the ground floor of a multistory building, had two bedrooms and a living room with shabby furniture, a kitchen, and a bathroom. Islam had paid the rent for them for one month up front. With only 300 LE (Egyptian pounds), the equivalent of $40, left in his pocket after paying for the family's passage to Cairo, Shokri was already worrying about how they would come up with the next month's rent.

The apartment was filthy, but Doaa and her family slept that night without bothering to clean or unpack; they were exhausted from their journey and not yet ready to face their new environment.

Doaa tossed and turned that first night. She was particular about cleanliness and kept imagining the dust on the floor rolling toward her in her sleep. The next morning, the family went out shopping at a local market looking for breakfast and some cleaning products. When they returned home, they all pitched in to sweep and scrub the apartment. It felt good to keep busy and have something to take their minds off their unease in their new surroundings. Doaa threw herself into cleaning, doing what she could to take control of her new situation.

In the afternoon, neighbors started stopping by the apartment with arms full of store-bought and homemade things to eat: salty Domiati cheese, fried chicken, steamed rice, trays of baklava, and baskets filled with fresh fruit. They were refugees as well from Damascus, Homs, and even some from Daraa. The Al Zamels quickly made friends with their neighbors, bonding over stories of the thrill of the revolution and the terror of war that had driven them from their country to Egypt. The atmosphere these people brought to the living room was festive and welcoming. Doaa found herself laughing and smiling with her new neighbors, relieved to be among her own people.

Doaa's family was part of the first wave of Syrians to flee to Egypt since the conflict began in 2011, most of whom came to join Syrian friends and family who were working there. Others had business connections or other personal networks that could offer them shelter. To get by, most refugees relied on personal savings, found odd jobs, or opened businesses, and many were able to become self-reliant. That was the hope of Doaa's parents, too, but soon after they arrived, a bigger influx of refugees brought more competition for work, making it harder to make ends meet. During the first half of 2013, the number of Syrian refugees rose dramatically. One year after the Al Zamels arrived in Egypt, the United Nations High Commissioner for Refugees (UNHCR) registered 125,499 Syrian refugees in the country, and according to the Egyptian government, that figure was actually closer to 300,000 if all unregistered Syrians were taken into account.

The supportive communities that formed among the refugees helped them get through the transition and helped ease Doaa's loneliness, although she missed home desperately. What if the move wasn't temporary? she often worried. What if she had to stay forever in this strange place? How would she ever adjust? She hated change.

The streets of their new neighborhood were filthy and smelled of decaying garbage. Stray dogs and cats ate from piled-up rubbish in the streets, and flies buzzed around the trash that seemed to be everywhere. Where were the streetlamps and the trash bins? Doaa would wonder as she wandered around town. The people of Daraa had prided themselves on the cleanliness of their city, and Doaa was shocked by the neglect in her new neighborhood. Gamasa did, however, have a lovely coastline and beach, and she was told that in the summer the city transformed into a resort for the working class. Looking around at the trash-filled streets, Doaa had a hard time believing it.

Feeling disconnected and homesick, Doaa spent a lot of time worrying about her family's future. She knew her father was running out of money fast. With her three older sisters, Alaa, Ayat, and Asma, married and in Abu Dhabi, Lebanon, and Syria, Doaa was now the eldest child in the family. This role carried responsibilities that she had no idea how to fulfill as she felt so helpless.

She knew that she and her family were now safe in Egypt and tried to convince herself that they were better off here. She tried to focus on the new sense of safety and normalcy and reveled in hearing everyday city-street sounds instead of shelling and bombs. But despite all this, Doaa had trouble ignoring the numbness that overcame her. At least in Daraa, she had a purpose. She was a recognized member of a supportive community that was standing up for values that were under attack. Here, she felt like a tolerated guest living off sympathy: a refugee and one of a growing group of helpless people. Even worse, she sometimes felt that she had abandoned her country, even though she knew that staying in Syria might have killed her. But who was she without her community? What meaningful contribution could she make here while her country was destroying itself? Doaa tried to not reveal her gloom to her family. She would often remind herself, *Be patient, this is a new challenge. Your family needs you to be strong for them. There is nothing more important to you than their well-being.*

One month after their arrival, the family's funds ran out, and the depression that had gripped Shokri after his shop was destroyed worsened. His cholesterol and blood pressure rose and he would spend hours sitting on a cushion in the common room, smoking or drinking sweetened tea, without moving or talking. Doaa felt that her father was slipping away from her. She knew that he thought that he'd failed his family, and he was too proud to talk about it. Her parents never complained or argued in front of them, but Doaa could clearly see how the pressures of their new life were affecting them, especially when it became clear that they might have to stay in Egypt even longer than they had anticipated. As they watched the news showing more clashes and bombings back home, Hanaa would say, "Thank goodness we left." Shokri, however, would insist that it wouldn't be long until they could return, reminding them of the period of transitions that occurred in Tunisia after the uprising, and in Egypt after the Muslim Brotherhood took control. As much as Doaa wanted to believe her father, she knew that it was his despair talking; everything she saw on the news made it clear they wouldn't be able to go home anytime soon.

Back in February 2011 a popular protest took place in Egypt ousting its autocratic president, Hosni Mubarak. Over time the Muslim Brotherhood gained popularity in the country and rose to power. The secular and non-Muslim populations of Egypt were deeply uncomfortable with this development, and in June 2012, a few months before Doaa and her family arrived in Damietta, the Muslim Brotherhood chairman, Mohamed Morsi, won the presidency with 51 percent of the vote in Egypt's first democratic election. Morsi promised to lead a government that would be "for all Egyptians," but his critics soon accused him of awarding key government positions to Islamists and criticized him for not introducing the economic and social reforms that he had promised during his campaign.

When Doaa's family first arrived in Egypt, they were mostly unaware of the public opposition that had begun to build against the Brotherhood and President Morsi within months of his taking office. The family were more preoccupied with the news from their own home country. To the Al Zamels, the Muslim Brotherhood's government was the one that had given them refuge and offered them much-needed help during a time of crisis. They also knew that Morsi was a vocal supporter of the Syrian opposition in its rebellion against President Assad. Up until then, the Al Zamels had had mainly positive interactions with the Egyptian government.

Officials from the local branch of the Muslim Brotherhood government made regular rounds to the buildings housing Syrian refugees to check in with them. After enduring the anxiety-inducing raids back in Syria, the first time Doaa's family heard knocking at their door, they all froze in fear, suspicious of any unexpected visitors. Doaa stood by her father, ready to offer her support, as he opened the door. Instead of aggressive soldiers with guns, they found two smiling men standing in the doorway, one holding a plastic bag, the other with an armful of warm blankets.

"You are welcome here. You are our brothers," they said, offering Shokri their goods. Doaa peered over her father's shoulder and discovered that the bag they held was filled with pasta, sugar, rice, and other staples. The man with the plastic bag handed it to Shokri, while the man with the blankets bent down to set them on the floor just inside the doorway. Shocked, Shokri stammered out his thanks.

While handouts like these were helpful, the family still had no money for rent. After two weeks, Shokri began to ask around for a cheaper place to live. To his astonishment, he heard of an Egyptian hotel owner who wanted to help Syrian refugees by offering free accommodation for the winter season while his hotel was empty. From May until October, the Gamasa neighborhood of Damietta was filled with working-class Egyptians who flocked to the beaches and cheap hotels along its Mediterranean shore for a summer vacation, but during the winter, the area was deserted.

Doaa and her family couldn't believe that someone would be offering a free place to stay, so Shokri went to check out the place. When he returned, he was optimistic. So the Al Zamels once again packed up their belongings and took a cheap three-wheeled tuk-tuk to Hotel Amira. It was on a dirt road, in sight of one of the biggest mosques in Gamasa. The blue and white paint was chipping off the picket fence, which had collapsed in places as if a car had driven into it. Khalid, the hotel manager, together with his wife and children, rushed out to greet them, inviting them to explore the grounds and to choose a family suite. They were the first Syrian-refugee guests in the hotel, so they could have their pick of the rooms.

Inside the hotel was more chipped paint, and the single beds creaked from wear and age. Meanwhile the appliances in the small kitchen and bathroom were cracked and rusty, but the rooms did have wide balconies that overlooked the hotel garden, where they could see green grass, a huge palm tree, sculpted bushes, and welcoming benches. The hotel was a haven of humanity to them, and they were deeply grateful. They chose a suite with two adjoining bedrooms, and Khalid handed over the keys.

The hotel owner, Fadlon, would stop by now and then, offering the family his sympathy and respect. Whenever the Al Zamels expressed their gratitude for his generosity, he always claimed that he was happy to help them, and every time he spotted nine-year-old Hamudi on his own, he would slip some bills into his hand, knowing that Shokri and Hanaa would be too proud to accept his cash. Word of Fadlon's generosity spread around town, and soon the hotel filled up with Syrian refugee families. In the afternoons, refugee guests gathered around a long wooden picnic table in the garden, exchanging stories about life before the war and the pain and suffering that followed. Locals and religious groups who sympathized with the Syrians dropped clothing and blankets off by the hotel. Time and time again, the people of Egypt made them feel welcome.

One evening after the Al Zamels had lived there for one month, Khalid invited them to his home for a meal. He, his wife, and their four sons lived about an hour's drive away in a small suburb called Kfar AlGhab. Khalid's wife cooked them a dinner of soup, salad, and duck with rice. After the meal, Khalid took them on a tour of his neighborhood and introduced them to neighbors as his Syrian friends. Khalid became the Al Zamels' first Egyptian friend, and for the first time since leaving Syria, Doaa felt a comforting sense of home.

As winter came to an end the hotel began to fill up with

guests, and Doaa and her family had to leave their haven. They searched for new accommodations, but this time they found no sympathetic building owner to help them. Landlords often price-gouged Syrian renters, taking advantage of their desperation.

Shokri earned a little money from odd jobs, but not much. The family soon moved into a small apartment in a noisy area of Gamasa that was littered with trash and piled with dirt from the unpaved road. Doaa's heart sank the first time she saw it. Noise assailed the family day and night as Egyptian vacationers stayed up late, playing music and talking loudly in the streets. Doaa often lay awake in bed, unable to sleep and yearning for the quiet nights of Daraa before the war.

While her sisters made friends with the girls in the neighborhood, Doaa sank into a depression, unable to eat and spending entire days in the dreary apartment watching news from Al Jazeera, Orient News TV, and the Free Syrian Army channel, aching to be home and taking part in the revolution. She desperately tried to make contact with her friends back in Syria, but the phone lines were mostly cut or jammed and she rarely got through. Occasionally, she managed to reach her sister Asma for just a few minutes on Skype.

One day Doaa received a message from her sister that filled her with worry. Asma read it out loud to her: "I miss you. The neighborhood misses you. It's hard to live here without you. The whole neighborhood is crying. You are the light of the neighborhood and it has gone dark without you." Back home, more people were dying every day, the supermarkets had almost nothing to sell, and each week more buildings were bombed to their foundations. Doaa begged her father to take them back to Syria where they could make a difference, rather than feeling useless in Egypt. Shokri looked at his daughter incredulously. "I am not bringing you back there to die," he said, dismissing her pleas. Doaa argued and begged, but Shokri stood firm.

When Shokri grew too ill to work, she and Saja decided that it was up to them to support the family. They couldn't start school until the next year, so they figured that they could use the free time to help their father, even though they were only seventeen and fifteen years old.

They found work in a factory that produced burlap bags. The owner told them that he wasn't actually short of workers— about one hundred men and a few women were already working there—but he wanted to do his part to help Syrians. Every morning, the girls took a 7:00 a.m. bus to the factory and spent the day sewing bags, counting them, and carrying them on their backs to a scale where they were weighed and then placed on a stack. Doaa, weighing just eighty-eight pounds, would struggle under her heavy load. The workdays were long and hard. They had only one break for noon prayer and then worked until late in the evening. They had nothing to eat during the day; only cups of tea were served at their workplace. Doaa and Saja were two of just a few young women working in the factory, but they were treated with respect and kindness by their coworkers.

The best part of the job was the friends they made there.

Doaa and Saja would whisper and joke with some of their young female Egyptian coworkers. One time one of them linked arms with Doaa and told her, "I love Bashar al-Assad because he gave us the chance to meet you." Doaa missed her school friends back in Daraa and savored any opportunity to have girls her age to talk to. It helped her imagine a time when she could maybe feel more at home in Egypt.

As Doaa settled into her work, she began to feel less helpless and dispossessed. She was now bringing home money for her family and earning the respect of the people she worked for. She no longer felt like someone who had run away from the fight for her country, but like a young woman who was taking care of and providing for her family. Every time she handed money to her parents, she felt pride lift her chest. Her mother noticed the difference in her daughter's attitude and felt a quiet satisfaction at watching her transform into a capable young woman.

Doaa also attracted the attention of the young men around her. During the three months she worked at the factory, two Egyptian men proposed to her, but she refused them both, despite being at an age at which girls often wed. Marriage was the last thing on Doaa's mind. When she did marry, she knew it would be to a Syrian man once she returned back home.

One day Doaa took a day off work to take care of her mother, who was sick. As she made her mother tea and took care of Hamudi, she worried that she might lose her job or that the owner would cut her pay, so when she returned to work the next day, she went straight to the shift manager and offered to make up the time.

She entered his office with her eyes lowered and apologized for missing work. But instead of scolding her, as she expected, he smiled kindly at her and asked for her home address. The following evening, the doorbell rang and the shift manager and his assistant stood there bearing a basket full of fruit and sweets, and asking for Hanaa. When they sat with the family, they said that they had come to wish her a quick recovery. "We love Syrians. You are welcome in our country and we stand by you," the shift manager told Hanaa and Shokri, leaning forward over his tea. "And don't worry about your girls at the factory. I am looking after them."

Doaa was touched.

At night, while Doaa relaxed from a hard day's work, her thoughts would return to Syria. She spent her evenings flipping through news channels, waiting for the segments about the war. She texted back and forth with her closest friend, Amal, who was still in Daraa, and asked for any news. Doaa told Amal how she wanted nothing more than to come back home. But Amal warned her, "It is better that you don't, Doaa, the situation is getting worse. It is dangerous for everybody. I don't even go to demonstrations anymore now that you're not here." Doaa's text conversations with Amal always left Doaa feeling conflicted. The danger of returning to Syria didn't frighten her, but leaving her family without her support did. She couldn't abandon them. She realized that she was needed here more than she was back there.

Meanwhile, Hanaa could tell that Doaa was longing for Syria, so Hanaa hid Doaa's passport and kept a close eye on her stubborn daughter. Hanaa saw text messages on Doaa's phone from friends back home that urged her to come back and rejoin their struggle. When Hanaa confronted her about the texts, Doaa assured her that she would not abandon the family. Hanaa then realized that in the months since Doaa had left Syria, she had matured. She had taken on responsibility for her family and was doing her part for them to get by in this life of exile, and that was all that mattered now.

However, the work at the factory was taking its toll on Doaa's health and she was becoming more fragile with each passing day. When she was anxious and tired, she couldn't eat, and her anemia returned. Shokri heard about a Syrian business owner, Mohamed Abu Bashir, who said that he could give all three of Shokri's daughters sewing work for 500 LE ($50) each per month—more than they got making burlap bags. They all quickly accepted the new jobs.

Mohamed had converted a small ground-floor apartment into work spaces for his ten employees, installing big industrial sewing machines and ironing boards in the bedrooms. Saja and Nawara worked the sewing machines to make skirts and pajamas, while Doaa was in charge of ironing.

The girls worked alone in one room and chatted and joked together as they worked. The boss made his rounds several times a day and would often single out Doaa for praise. This made her feel useful and appreciated in her job, despite the fact that the girls' paychecks never quite added up to 500 LE after some mysterious deductions were made by the owner.

Though Doaa still longed for Syria, after six months she

was slowly beginning to find her place in Egypt and was accepting her family's fate. They had just enough income to cover rent, and with the food vouchers from UNHCR, they were able to buy ingredients for the meals Hanaa prepared. They also slowly paid off the debts they owed to those in the Syrian community who had helped them when they first arrived.

Doaa realized that the longer she stayed in Egypt, the more she felt her old dreams slipping away from her. In Syria, before the war, she was on a path to go to university. She still had one more year of high school left, but now she had no meaningful way to continue her education in Egypt. The best she could do was to attend some classes at a school run by Syrian teachers during the local school's afternoon shift for refugee students.

Doaa tried to comfort herself by thinking of the progress she and her family had made in Egypt. While they didn't have much, their situation had improved, and the constant tension that they had felt in Syria began to ease. Little Hamudi, who, when they'd first arrived in Gamasa, would never leave Hanaa's side, began to make friends and sleep peacefully through the night, his nightmares and anxiety finally receding. Doaa told herself that for now all she wanted was peace and happiness and food on the table for her family.

FIVE

Love in Exile

After six months as refugees, the Al Zamel family was growing accustomed to life in Egypt. Doaa's sister Asma and her two young daughters were now there with them. Asma had left Daraa to join the family when the bombing intensified, turning their neighborhood into a death zone. Asma's husband, however, despite her pleas to him to leave with them, stayed behind to fight for the Free Syrian Army.

Growing numbers of Syrians were fleeing the country to stay alive, and also finding refuge in Egypt, including in Damietta. On weekends, when the Al Zamels took strolls along the seaside walkway, also known as the Corniche, just like the Egyptian families, passersby clearly saw that they were outsiders, but understood that war had driven them here, and they were accepted. On these walks, the eyes of the Al Zamels would occasionally meet the eyes of others, and their heads would nod in acknowledgment, as if they were telling the family,

"We feel for you." Syrian women were easily recognizable by the way they wore their veil differently from Egyptian women. So men would often call out to them, "You are welcome here!" And sometimes they would call out in jest, "Will you marry me?"

As news from home trickled in, the Al Zamels accepted that they would be staying in Egypt much longer than they had originally thought. Friends from Daraa told them that some of their neighbors had been killed in the struggle, and that their once bustling neighborhood was now deserted. Not long after Asma fled Syria, her house was hit by a missile and the house across the street was reduced to rubble. Doaa's family worried about the friends who were left behind and sent daily text messages to them, checking to see if they were still alive. Doaa searched the news in vain for signs of a break in the violence and a return to peace so she could go home.

In early May, six months after their arrival in Egypt, Doaa's twenty-four-year-old cousin, Maisam, had news. Maisam and his wife, who had arrived in Egypt two months after the Al Zamels, lived in an apartment upstairs. One day he sat next to Hanaa, sipping tea, and announced excitedly, "My best friend, Bassem, is coming to stay with us, you'll love him, Aunt Hanaa! Everyone who knew him in Daraa did."

Bassem was twenty-eight years old and, up until the war, had a thriving downtown hairdressing salon that he'd bought with his own savings. When the war started in Daraa and his business was shut down, he joined the opposition and began fighting for the FSA. Eventually, he was caught. During his two months in jail, he was tortured, tied up by his hands, forced to sleep sitting up, and deprived of water. Maisam suspected that Bassem had endured even worse, but he refused to talk about it. When he was finally released, he learned that his brother, also a fighter for the FSA, had been killed while carrying Bassem's ID card in his wallet. Because of this Bassem was no longer just a guy with a record, but someone the government had probably registered as an enemy killed in combat. Without a valid ID, it was impossible to pass through the army checkpoints that dotted the entire city. Bassem was already under scrutiny after prison, but now his life would be in greater danger every time he left home.

Maisam had convinced his friend to leave Syria before he suffered the same fate as his brother. Maisam told Hanaa that Bassem was due to arrive in just a few days.

Several nights later, Maisam called Hanaa and asked her to prepare a meal. "Today is a holiday," he proclaimed. "My friend Bassem is here!" Hanaa instructed Doaa to warm up some leftovers and bring them upstairs since Maisam's wife, Shifaa, was pregnant with twins and needed the help.

Doaa did as she was told and carefully carried some plates of hot food up a flight of stairs to Maisam and Shifaa's apartment. Shifaa opened the door and smiled gratefully at Doaa when she saw the plates of food. "Thank you!" she gushed, giving Doaa a quick hug. "And tell your mother thank you. I can barely move, much less cook!" Doaa kissed Shifaa's cheek, smiled down at her huge belly, then nodded to her cousin Maisam, catching a glimpse of the new visitor.

The first time Doaa saw Bassem, she was not particularly impressed. Modesty and custom prevented her from looking directly at a strange man. So as she entered the room, she kept her eyes lowered and went about quickly placing the dishes of food on a cloth in the center of the floor where the places were set. Doaa managed to steal a quick look at the young man's profile and found him unremarkable.

After a few minutes, she excused herself, telling Maisam and Shifaa that she had to help Asma and her daughters pack because they were moving to Jordan the next day. Since Asma's husband was still in Syria, they had decided to settle back in Irbid to be closer to him. Doaa hugged Shifaa, left the apartment, and promptly forgot all about Maisam's young refugee friend.

The next morning, Shokri, Doaa, and her sisters helped Asma carry her heavy bags down five flights of stairs and loaded them into a taxi for the four-hour trip to the Alexandria airport.

Once at the check-in counter, officials looked at Asma's ticket and noticed that it was one-way, but that she didn't have a visa. They told her that the only way she could leave would be if she bought a return ticket for an additional $500. Asma burst into tears when she heard this news. She didn't have that much money. Shokri explained to the airline official that they were poor refugees and that his daughter needed to rejoin her husband. "Let her go and we will pay later, please," he begged.

The airline employee softened when he heard this and said,

"You can have two days to get the money. I'll change your ticket, just bring the cash." Asma texted her husband in Syria, alerting him to what had happened and asking him to wire money, and the family made the long journey back home.

Back at the apartment, Doaa and each of her sisters grabbed a bag and struggled to haul them up the long flights of stairs to the apartment. Bassem entered the stairwell as Doaa, the last in the group, was lifting and dropping a suitcase one step at a time up the stairs. She was wearing a red veil, one of her favorites, and a long, flowing dress. Her face was flushed from the exertion.

"Can I help you?" Bassem asked as he reached out to take the suitcase. Seeing his gesture, Doaa held on more tightly to the handle and politely refused. Bassem, struck by the sight of this slight woman determinedly hauling a heavy suitcase up a flight of stairs, tried to insist, but that only made Doaa more adamant that she could do it herself. "I can manage just fine alone," she said curtly. She wasn't used to talking to men she didn't know, but she also took pride in her ability to handle her own affairs and hated the idea of anyone pitying her, especially because she was a girl. She wouldn't let a man she barely knew think she was weak. She continued to stubbornly drag the suitcase, step by step, up to the apartment.

Doaa didn't think much of the episode, but Bassem was left enchanted. He rushed up to Maisam's apartment, breathing hard from the climb, but also out of excitement, and asked, "What is the name of your beautiful cousin with the red veil?"

Maisam answered, "That's Doaa! I told you that the night you arrived when she brought up our food. Or maybe that was Saja? I forget."

"Is she engaged?"

Maisam grinned. "No." Then thinking twice, he responded, "Neither of them is."

"Good. I want her to be mine." Bassem smiled. "There's something about her. She has completely captivated me."

Maisam shrugged, thinking that his friend had become a hopeless romantic, but glad to see him excited about something. Pursuing Doaa would be a good diversion for him, Maisam thought, as he watched Bassem move around the apartment with a new spring in his step.

Bassem had been solemn and reticent since he'd arrived in Egypt. He wouldn't talk about what had happened in prison or of the death of his brother. He seemed to want to keep that experience cloistered away and to move on. If courting Doaa helped him get by, Maisam would help in whatever way he could.

A few days later, Bassem and Maisam packed up the few belongings in their apartment to move. Maisam and Shifaa had found a different building that had an equally affordable flat for rent on a lower floor, so Shifaa would have an easier time getting around once the twins were born. They invited Bassem to move with them.

Once they all settled into their new home, they invited the Al Zamel family to come visit for lunch. When Bassem answered the door, Doaa noticed that he had dressed for the occasion, wearing a crisply ironed shirt and dress trousers. His black hair was slicked back with gel, and a pronounced goatee protruded from his trimmed beard—a modern look. He fixed his dark almond eyes on Doaa's the moment she entered the room, and throughout the meal he kept the conversation animated, making the guests laugh. Doaa kept feeling his gaze return to her, as if seeking her acknowledgment and approval.

On their walk home, Doaa turned to her sisters, asking, "Why was he looking at us like that?"

"I think he fancies you!" Saja said, grinning. Thinking that Saja just had an active imagination, Doaa made a face at her little sister.

The following day, Maisam came by the Al Zamel apartment for his regular afternoon visit. As Doaa made tea in the kitchen, Maisam sauntered in. Leaning against the counter, he grabbed a biscuit from a plate and said, "Hey, Frog," using his nickname for her, "what do you think of Bassem?"

Doaa gave him a blank stare. She hadn't thought much about him at all.

At Doaa's silence Maisam exclaimed, "Doaa! Bassem is seriously taken with you. He wants to propose to you!"

Hearing this, Doaa set down the teapot she was filling and looked at her cousin in shock. "What? So quickly? He's only seen me twice." In traditional Arab culture when a couple got engaged, they entered into a formal arrangement that allowed them to openly date and then decide if they were meant for marriage. But Doaa wasn't interested in any of this.

"Twice was enough to convince him of his feelings for you."

Maisam began to make a case for his friend. "Listen, Doaa, Bassem's a hard worker. He was successful back home. He has savings, and here he will be sure to get a good job."

Doaa shook her head. "Bassem knows nothing about me, and in any case I'm not interested. Please let him know politely," she said, thinking that would be the end of it. But deep down, Doaa was annoyed with Maisam, thinking that he was the one encouraging Bassem to propose so quickly. She felt put off by what seemed to her like a scheme that her cousin had concocted. She didn't speak to Maisam for a week after their discussion.

Maisam went home and told his friend what had happened, gently suggesting that maybe he should look for someone else. Doaa was set in her ways, and she had made it clear that she wasn't interested. Bassem took the rejection hard. According to everyone who knew him, his actions came straight from his heart. He was deeply passionate, whether fighting for his country or falling in love, but he was also fiercely protective of the people he cared about, and from the moment he first saw Doaa, he wanted to take care of her. He had arrived in Egypt alone and in grief, and Doaa was the first glimmer of light in the dark of his refugee life. In her he saw a hope for the future. He was immediately convinced that she was the one person who could make him happy. He'd never felt that way about a girl before. He was also confounded by her refusal. Doaa was also the first girl to ever turn him down. In the past girls had always approached him. He left Maisam's apartment that day upset.

Over the next few days, Bassem did nothing but sit around

the apartment feeling depressed. Maisam and Shifaa did their best to console him, urging him to be patient. He couldn't expect a girl he'd just met to accept him right away. However, Maisam genuinely believed that Doaa and Bassem would make a good match, so he offered to speak to Hanaa on Bassem's behalf. She could surely talk some sense into her daughter.

Hanaa was taken aback by the news at first, but then reconfirmed for Maisam that her daughter was not interested in being engaged to anyone. However, she did promise to talk to Doaa about Bassem. But when she brought up the subject, Doaa was annoyed. "I already told Maisam that I have no interest in his friend, Mama, and on top of that, no interest in marriage either!" Doaa had other things on her mind. She was working long hours to support the family, and the rest of her time was occupied with contacting her friends back home for updates on the situation in Syria. And she had her own dreams for the future that she hoped to get back on track.

"How can I get engaged to him, Mama? I didn't leave our country just to get married without finishing my studies."

"Of course, my dear." Hanaa offered Doaa a hug. "I understand and support you."

Relieved to have her mother on her side, Doaa considered the matter closed. Bassem was not the first man to propose to her, and besides, she didn't think that he was serious about her anyway. The other men who had proposed had not been serious either; they had all given up right away once she had said no, and she'd gone right back to her work at the sewing factory.

Bassem, however, did not give up; instead he began to form

a plan. He convinced Maisam to give him Hanaa's phone number so he could speak to her directly. The first time Bassem phoned, he explained to Hanaa that he just wanted her to have his number in case she ever needed anything. But then, he started calling her daily, sometimes asking about Doaa, other times merely inquiring about the family. Hanaa liked Bassem, and the more she got to know him, the more her sympathy for him grew. He was smart, strong, devoted, and good-hearted—just like Doaa. Hanaa began to think that he was the perfect match for her headstrong daughter. She knew Doaa was stubborn and that it was hard for her to trust people. When Doaa was a little girl, that obstinacy and fear had kept her from making new friends, and now Hanaa feared that it would keep her from opening up to the possibility of love.

Three months after Bassem and Doaa first met, he approached Hanaa. "I saw Doaa coming home from work, and she looked so exhausted. Please get her to stop working," he pleaded. "I will give you whatever she was earning to make up for it."

Hanaa had heard about how generous Bassem was with other Syrians, paying their expenses and buying them things that they needed. In the refugee community, people took care of one another, and Hanaa was touched by Bassem's offer to help the family and Doaa, but when Doaa found out, she was furious. She hated that someone thought she was weak; it was crucial to her that people knew that she could take care of herself and her family and that she didn't need anyone's help to do so. When Hanaa told her of Bassem's offer, Doaa was angry even though she knew that she was more than exhausted. She was having dizzy spells almost daily and fainted regularly. She often found it difficult to eat after a long day of work, but despite all this, she had no intention of accepting handouts. Bassem's offer made her all the more determined to carry on with her job.

"I feel fine," she insisted, trying to ignore the fainting episodes, constant dizziness, and the depression that was beginning to creep up on her.

It seemed that everyone in Gamasa knew that Bassem was in love with Doaa, and that she had rejected his proposal. He soon became known around town as Romeo Bassem. Doaa's sisters liked Bassem and ended up taking his side. They tried to persuade Doaa to change her mind and accept his proposal. Even the owner of the factory where Doaa worked interrupted her ironing one day and asked, "Why don't you want to marry Bassem?" All this just made Doaa more entrenched in refusing him. She hated being told what to do.

"I cannot love him," she told her family. "And, anyway, I don't want to get married outside of Syria."

Doaa's outright refusal of Bassem worried Hanaa. She feared that Doaa's fatigue and depression were making her shut out any possibility of love or happiness. Hanaa's once ebullient daughter was now always grim and serious. Hanaa knew that she could never force Doaa into anything, but felt a responsibility as Doaa's mother to push past her stubborn daughter's barriers on this. Hanaa had gotten to know Bassem well by now from all his phone calls and walks in the neighborhood, and she trusted his sincerity. She began to get annoyed with Doaa's obstinacy.

"He is Syrian!" Hanaa countered. "And he is a kind person who wants to help you, Doaa. Please open your heart to him."

Doaa felt that everyone was ganging up on her. She didn't see why she should accept Bassem's proposal just because people thought she should. When she found out that he had found a nice ground-floor apartment in his building for her family to consider moving into, she felt as if this were all part of some big plot to make her accept him. She continued to refuse him and to make the best life that she could in Egypt on her own. But that life was about to get much harder.

Doaa and her family hadn't been paying close attention to the Egyptian news since they were too busy watching the daily horror show that was the destruction of their own country. But on June 30, 2013, the first anniversary of the inauguration of President Morsi, mass demonstrations in Cairo and Alexandria against his rule had reached a level that they couldn't ignore. Growing frustration and disenchantment with the government brought millions of people to the streets, complaining that the revolution that had brought down President Mubarak two years before had now been hijacked. Living standards were deteriorating, secular politicians were being alienated from their own government, and Morsi's draft constitution had an Islamist slant that troubled much of the population. Egyptians began to worry their country could unravel violently the same way that Syria had. The protests in Egypt continued for four days. Then, on July 3, 2013, eight months after the Al Zamels had arrived in Damietta, Mohamed Morsi was ousted by the army. General Abdel Fattah el-Sisi orchestrated the coup that swept Morsi out of power, and overnight, attitudes toward Syrian refugees in the country changed, swept up in the same wave that overthrew Morsi and the Muslim Brotherhood. Since Morsi had been welcoming to Syrian refugees, people believed they were part of his movement and were his supporters.

Doaa's family could do nothing but watch as Egyptian news anchors began to label Syrians as potential terrorists who were allied with the extremists that were emerging in Syria. And if they weren't terrorists, then they were considered Morsi supporters. Allegations arose that the Muslim Brotherhood had paid Syrian refugees to join demonstrations in support of Morsi. Youssef el-Husseini, a well-known state TV talk show host, delivered an ominous message to Syrians: "If you are a man, you should return to your country and solve your problem there. If you interfere in Egypt, you will be beaten by thirty shoes." In Middle Eastern culture, hitting someone with a shoe is considered to be belittling, and to Syrians, hearing this threat was both frightening and insulting. Egypt's open-door policy came to an end with an announcement that a visa would be required for any Syrian to enter the country, and any Syrians already in Egypt who didn't have the proper residency paperwork would be arrested and possibly deported.

The atmosphere in Egypt for Syrians changed dramatically during this time. They got no more friendly greetings in the streets, just cold stares. The aid they used to receive from the local Muslim Brotherhood community dried up, and instead locals in the street told them that they were ruining the country.

The girls began to get harassed whenever they left the house. One day, Doaa was walking to the supermarket with her mother when a man on a motorbike slowed down and rode close to them. He leaned over, almost touching Doaa, and taunted, "Hey, girl, would you marry me?" Then to Hanaa, he called, "Would you let me marry her? She is very beautiful." He leered at Doaa, ogling her body up and down and making kissing sounds. Doaa could smell his sour breath and recoiled from him, disgusted and afraid. The man circled them twice on his motorbike, then drove away, laughing at their fear. Doaa and her family had been aware that sexual harassment was pervasive in Egypt but had never experienced it themselves, and now it seemed that it was predominantly directed at Syrian women. Doaa and her sisters no longer felt safe in their neighborhood. What had once been a country of refuge was now just one more place of menace for Doaa and her family.

Bassem, meanwhile, had grown desperate in his love for Doaa. One day, one of his flatmates came to the Al Zamel apartment to tell Hanaa that he thought Bassem was going to kill himself if he couldn't marry Doaa and that he'd seen a bottle of poison in Bassem's room. When Hanaa went to check on him, at the door he wouldn't meet her eyes. Bassem had become pale and thin, and Hanaa pushed her way past him and into his room and found the bottle of rat poison.

Furious, she scolded him, "You can't do this to yourself." She waved the bottle in his face. "Men can't be like this."

He looked down at the ground, ashamed. He told her he didn't want to live if he couldn't be with Doaa. "I'm going back to Syria to fight if she does not accept my proposal. There's nothing else here for me."

From the quiet certainty about him when he told her this, Hanaa believed that he would actually do it. Bassem already felt like a son to her, and she couldn't bear the thought of his dying in the war. She tried to encourage him to have faith: "Be patient! Maybe she'll change her mind, but in the meantime you must be strong."

Hanaa took the bottle of rat poison with her when she left, promising to check back in on him, then promptly threw the bottle away.

When Hanaa returned home that evening, she sat Doaa down in the common room and described to Doaa the lengths Bassem was prepared to go to convince her of his love, including taking his own life. She took Doaa's cold hands in hers. Doaa's hands were always icy when she felt exhausted or worked too hard. "When a man humiliates himself for a woman, it means he truly loves her," Hanaa said. "Will you at least think about accepting his engagement?"

Hearing about Bassem's desperation made Doaa feel guilty. She didn't want him to be miserable, but she also didn't like the pressure his actions put her under. "I don't deserve this," she told her mother, "and I don't want his love." Saja, overhearing, interjected, "I wish someone would do that for me. He must really love you." But Doaa ignored her sister. She refused to be pressured or cajoled into accepting any man.

The following day, when Doaa left the apartment, she was surprised to see Bassem dressed in a new suit with his hair freshly groomed, smelling of aftershave. "Doaa," he said, "I know what I did was wrong. You don't deserve that kind of pressure. Please forgive me."

At that moment Doaa finally began to soften toward Bassem, wondering if it was only her own stubbornness that kept her from liking him. As she accepted his apology, she found herself tongue-tied and as shy as she had been as a little girl. All she could bring herself to say was "Thank you for coming."

A few days later, one sweltering July evening, Doaa suddenly felt faint. The next thing she knew her feet had left the ground and her head knocked against the floor. She didn't know at first that when Hanaa found her unconscious at home alone, the first person she thought to call was Bassem. He instructed her to go to a private hospital. "Avoid a public hospital at all costs," he warned. "I'll cover any expenses." The public hospitals were notorious for providing terrible care, and sometimes no care at all; patients could wait for hours without being seen. So Hanaa and her sister, Feryal, who was visiting at the time, carefully led a half-conscious Doaa to a taxi and gave the address for a private clinic. Bassem arrived shortly after. He bluffed his way inside, telling the hospital staff that he was family, and found his way into her room. He immediately took charge. He found a pharmacy and bought the medication that Doaa needed. The doctor told the family that Doaa's health was precarious. She was too thin and frail, and in such a weakened state, she was vulnerable to any number of dangerous illnesses. When he told the family she would need to rest and be cared for, and that her health would need to be monitored carefully, Bassem insisted that he would do whatever was needed to take care of Doaa.

"I will pay for Doaa to see the best doctors in Alexandria, or even Cairo. I'll use all my savings to make sure she's well," he told her mother.

Something inside Doaa shifted when she awoke and heard from her mother what Bassem had done for her. She heard from her sisters that he had been pacing nervously in the waiting room, asking a lot of concerned questions, while they waited for her diagnosis. Doaa lay in her hospital bed thinking about the young man who was willing to go to such lengths for her. His dedication convinced Doaa that his affection was genuine. She was used to being the one who took care of people, not the one being taken care of. A new feeling began to stir inside her, something she'd never felt before. For the first time since she'd been forced to flee her homeland, she felt her heart begin to open. What she was feeling though was more than compassion. Fondness, perhaps? Gratitude? It couldn't be love. She was certain of that.

The day Doaa was released from the hospital, about an hour after she arrived home, Hanaa's phone rang. It was Bassem. He asked to speak to Doaa. Doaa surprised herself by how eagerly she pulled the phone from her mother's hand to her own ear. "I just want to say thank you," she said shyly, then handed the phone back to her mother.

Not long afterward, Doaa returned to work, in spite of the

doctor's warning. She still felt responsible for taking care of her family and wanted to contribute. While she felt safe with her Syrian employer, the new anti-Syrian attitude in Egypt deeply affected her. Her father was losing clients at the barbershop he had begun working in, and with the added stress, she started feeling lethargic, sleeping a lot and, when awake, staring into space thinking of how their suffering had doubled: They had endured the war in Syria and now the Egyptian people were rejecting them. One night when she couldn't sleep, she watched her sleeping family, all the while feeling crushed by anxiety and despair. *There is no future for us,* she thought. No matter how hard she worked, she couldn't give her family a future. She felt the weight of the world on her thin shoulders and it kept her up all night.

One day, she fainted at work, and when she awoke in the public hospital, the doctor informed her that she had severe anemia and told her that she had to stay home for at least one month, eat well, and relax.

Doaa reluctantly took time off work to follow the doctor's orders, but during that time she had no appetite. She didn't care about getting healthy again. From her balcony, she could see Bassem leave for work at the hair salon in the morning and return in the evening. Her sisters told her stories about how when he saw them in the street, he would buy them small gifts and always ask about Doaa.

While all the women in the house and many neighbors knew about Bassem's feelings for Doaa, Shokri somehow remained oblivious. Hanaa and the girls had kept the drama from him—but he knew Bassem and often mentioned how much he liked him. Hanaa was becoming increasingly impatient with Doaa—and concerned. She didn't tell Doaa about Bassem's plan to return to Syria to fight, but she fretted about it and increased the pressure on Doaa to accept him. She told Doaa that her poor health was probably caused by her stubbornness, and that Bassem could bring her happiness and take care of her. Hanaa implored her to think about the engagement again, to open her heart, and to pray if it helped her, then to make a decision once and for all.

Doaa did pray for help. She knew her mother only wanted what was best for her, and she didn't fully understand why the thought of accepting Bassem upset her so much. She asked Allah what course she should take. Night after night, she prayed, but no answer came.

One night, Hanaa called Doaa over to sit beside her. Looking uncharacteristically unstable and weary, Hanaa asked point-blank, "Why don't you like Bassem? He's a great guy and he supports us." Doaa knew that her mother was right and couldn't give her a good answer; instead she looked away embarrassed. Hanaa took Doaa's chin in her hand and forced her to meet her eyes. "Enough is enough," she stated urgently. Doaa didn't quite understand what, but she could tell something was unnerving her mother.

A few hours later, when Doaa got ready for bed, she knelt for her prayers, then called out to her mother in the next bedroom to say her usual good-night. When she was met with silence, she called out again. Her mother always answered her, but not this time. A sense of panic and dread washed over her as Doaa quickly got to her feet and hurried to her parents' room, pounding her cold bare feet on the hard floor. She found her mother sitting in a trancelike state with her hand over her eyes, trembling uncontrollably and breathing harshly. Doaa shook her father awake, and together they carried Hanaa out the apartment door and into the street to hail a cab, while Hanaa moaned softly and could barely stand.

Bassem was sitting on his balcony at the time, enjoying a cigarette. When he noticed the family, he shouted down to them, asking what was wrong.

Doaa, crying in fear for her mother, called back up to him, "She's not well at all, she's barely conscious! We're taking her to the hospital!" The concern in Bassem's eyes warmed Doaa for a brief moment as they stepped into the taxi and sped away.

The doctor examined Hanaa and told the family that she was mentally and physically exhausted. She needed rest and the family had to care for her. Such a state was not uncommon in refugee patients, he said, after what they went through in Syria and now in Egypt. "She should not be given any bad news," he warned. "She might not be able to take it." Doaa felt as if the doctor were staring straight at her when he said this, and that her mother's illness was somehow linked to her rejection of Bassem and her mother's worry for her.

It was dawn by the time they returned home. Hanaa's phone

rang almost immediately upon their arrival, and Doaa noticed Bassem's name on the caller ID. She picked it up.

"I am so sorry," he said, "but I think I know why your
mother is sick! It's because of us."

Doaa was surprised that he had arrived at the same con-
clusion that she had. "Yes," she replied, her voice catching. She
couldn't bear to be the cause of her mother's illness. "It is our
fault."

Before she could say more, he blurted out, "Doaa, I want
to tell you something that I have only told your mother. I have
decided to return to Syria to fight with the opposition. If I die,
at least I know I will have you in heaven since I can't have you
in this life. I'm not leaving yet. I'll wait for your mother to get
better so I can say good-bye, but I am leaving in a few days."

Doaa was stunned at this news. She now understood why
her mother had been so upset. Hanaa had come to care deeply
for Bassem, even to love him as a son. "Now I know for sure
we are the reason she got sick!" she told Bassem, feeling suddenly as if she were confiding in a close friend. "It was because
she was so upset knowing that you would go back to Syria.
That's why she's been so angry with me lately." Doaa stood in
the doorway of her mother's room, watching Hanaa's chest
move up and down as she slept. Doaa leaned against the wall
outside her parents' room and held the phone pressed tightly
to her ear. She realized that she didn't want Bassem to hang
up, and that she hated the idea of not being able to talk to him
if he left Egypt.

Bassem's voice softened. "Doaa, do you think you could change your mind?" he asked hopefully. "Try and think about it more, but do it quickly. I'm going to leave in a few days. On Thursday at the latest. I can't stand to stay here any longer than that." Thursday was only three days away. Doaa thought about how much he cared for her and her family. FSA fighters died every day, and if he left, he could die, too.

"Give me some time and I'll call you back," Doaa promised as tears rolled down her face. When they hung up, Doaa wasn't sure if he had heard her crying.

Doaa agonized over her decision. Would Bassem really go back? Could he die because of her? Part of her admired him for having the courage to return to Syria to rejoin the struggle. Hadn't she fantasized about doing the same thing?

Word spread quickly of Bassem's imminent departure, and people whispered to each other about how he was leaving because he couldn't bear the pain of his broken heart.

Over the next few days Doaa couldn't stop thinking about him. She didn't want him to die because of her. Two days after their phone call, Doaa paced nervously around her apartment. She thought about Bassem's kind brown eyes and how much he had cared for her and her family. All of a sudden, she realized that maybe she didn't have to do everything alone. Her mother and father supported each other and they were stronger because of it. She admitted to herself that she couldn't stand the idea of not having Bassem around. Her Gamasa neighborhood would be dull and colorless again without him.

Doaa picked up her mobile and called Bassem.

"Nice to hear your voice, Doaa," he greeted her, before asking anxiously, "Did you think about it more?"

Without preparation, the words sputtered out of her mouth, "How come you say that you love me and yet you want to leave me and go to Syria?" she challenged.

Bassem replied just as quickly, "Because I'm burning with love for you, and I can't stand seeing you and not having you in my life. I'd rather become a martyr in Syria. The pain of not having you is too much to bear."

As if her voice belonged to someone else, she heard herself say, "Well, I've thought about it a lot, and if you are still interested, you can go and ask my father for my hand." As soon as she spoke the words, she knew she was speaking from her heart. Her fear of trusting someone was nothing compared to her fear of losing the man who might be the love of her life.

Bassem was dumbfounded by Doaa's response. "Are you sure you really mean it?"

"I mean it."

"Okay. Hang up the phone right now!" he screamed with jubilance. "I am going to your father's salon right now to ask for your hand! After that, I'll come right over!"

"No, silly." Doaa laughed. "You can't go right now. It's too late. Go tomorrow!"

Long after she hung up, she kept the phone in her hand thinking about the possibility of a new life ahead of her.

SIX

The Engagement

The next day, Shokri looked up from sweeping up after a client to see Bassem walking into the barbershop trailed by a group of friends. Bassem was wearing a good suit that was freshly pressed, his hair was carefully combed, and his beard was neatly trimmed.

Shokri smiled in welcome and offered the young men seats, but they all stayed standing while Bassem shifted nervously from one foot to the other.

"I came here to let you know that I have proposed to Doaa," he said at last. "I am here to ask for your support."

Shokri was incredulous. "Bassem, I like you very much. But Doaa doesn't want to get married." Shaking his head, Shokri went back to sweeping.

Bassem was baffled and didn't know how to respond to Shokri's dismissal. After a few awkward moments, one of his friends spoke up for him. "Bassem is serious, sir! He has been in love with Doaa for three months now!"

Shokri thought he knew his daughter well enough to know what her answer would be. He looked up from his work and answered with conviction, "Look, this is nothing personal, but I am quite sure that Doaa has no interest in getting engaged."

"B-b-but," Bassem stuttered, "she has agreed! It's true she didn't want to for a time, but she's changed her mind now."

Hearing this, Shokri brightened. He couldn't believe it, and he couldn't imagine a better match for Doaa than this hard-working, caring young man. Feeling suddenly optimistic and looking forward to something to celebrate, he smiled at Bassem. "Well, if Doaa wants this, I will of course agree to it."

Thrilled, Bassem immediately called Doaa to share the news. They set a date for their engagement ceremony for a few days later, August 28, 2013, and planned to throw a party to celebrate on September 1.

Bassem visited the family every day after work, bringing small gifts and lingering after dinner to sit beside Doaa and whisper to her. During his breaks from work, he called Doaa and sent her text messages with heart emojis and poems by his favorite Syrian poets.

Doaa and Bassem's engagement lifted a cloud from over the Al Zamel house. Hanaa's health improved and the new couple became the talk of the neighborhood. Everyone knew that Romeo Bassem had finally won his Juliet. The engagement was a bright spot in the midst of the everyday struggles of life as a refugee.

The first step in the engagement was the signing ceremony, a formal event witnessed by a small group of family and friends in the Al Zamels' home. Doaa, dressed in a black dress with a black-and-red veil, stood with the women on one side of a window, while Bassem and the men stood on the other side on a balcony. A sheikh, a local religious leader, laid out the contract—called the Katb el-Kitab—an Islamic prenuptial agreement that would sanction their relationship, and asked Doaa through the window three times if she took Bassem for her betrothed. Each time she replied resolutely, "I do." These responses made them man and wife in the eyes of God, then they signed the Katb el-Kitab. Afterward, Doaa joined Bassem on the balcony, while the family cheered them on, and Hanaa and the girls served tea and cake to all the guests. Later, they would need to visit a courthouse to make their engagement official. But for now they were blessed as a couple with the intention to marry, giving them the freedom to walk in public hand in hand.

Two days later, Bassem picked up Doaa, her sisters, and Hanaa to go buy Doaa some jewelry in preparation for the engagement celebration party. Traditionally, a man buys a ring, bracelets, earrings, a watch, and a necklace for his betrothed. But Doaa and Hanaa tried to convince Bassem that one piece of jewelry was enough. They knew that his savings were running out and his earnings were small. But he insisted on one of each, asking for the most expensive kind of gold. Doaa chose a necklace, earrings, and double ring and skipped the watch. The label on the ring was *Tag Elmalika,* or "a queen's crown." "That is just how you treat her," Hanaa said to Bassem, "like your queen."

For the engagement party Doaa bought a dress of a shiny sky-blue material with a tight bodice and full skirt. It had taken her days to find it, going from shop to shop with her mother.

Now that they had taken their vows together, Bassem and Doaa were allowed to go out alone together holding hands. He took her to cafés and out shopping to spoil her. After living so simply for so long, Doaa enjoyed being indulged. "I love how you dress," Bassem would tell her, joking that all the men were jealous of him to have such an elegant future wife. He also knew that she liked eating chips and sweets, so he would buy her little bags at kiosks for small picnics in the neighborhood garden. Bassem and Doaa would often go on strolls and visit a playground together where they would head for the swing set, like adolescents, giggling and whispering back and forth. "You are the best thing that ever happened to me, Dodo," he said, using his new nickname for her. "You can't know how much you made me suffer."

The morning of the party, Hanaa escorted Doaa to a hairdresser. Doaa's long hair went down to her waist, and the stylist spent well over an hour creating an intricate style that wrapped around her head, while a makeup artist transformed her face. Finally, with full makeup and hair, Doaa no longer looked like a downtrodden refugee or a factory girl. She looked and felt like a woman in love who could now look to a future that might not be so bleak.

Doaa was happy that she and Bassem had finally sanctioned their relationship and were now man and wife in the eyes of their religion, but in the taxi on the way home, she could not hold back her sadness at the thought that her older sisters could not be with her on her special day. Alaa, Ayat, and Asma were spread throughout the region: Alaa in Abu Dhabi, Ayat in Lebanon, and Asma in Jordan. As refugees, their Syrian passports were useless without visas. So they were stuck in the countries they had fled to and couldn't come to celebrate Doaa's engagement. Doaa wept at the unfairness of it, ruining her makeup.

When she emerged from a taxi at 4:00 p.m., after freshening up at home and fixing her mascara, over one hundred guests, both Syrians and Egyptians, were gathered to cheer for her. Bassem's friends set off fireworks, and the guests entered Doaa's aunt's apartment, where an array of home-cooked dishes, sweets, and bottles of fruit juice covered the tables. Doaa had charged Saja with decorating the space, and she, Nawara, and Doaa's aunts had built a small podium for the ceremony and bought streamers, balloons, and paper tablecloths. Flowers were everywhere, on tables, the podium, even the curtains, and every foot of the living room was decorated with celebratory color. The girls had cut out the initials D and B and pasted them on the wall for guests to see as they entered.

Doaa was swept in with the crowd and brought to her aunt's bedroom, to where the women had retreated. Arabic pop music played from a speaker system they had rented from a local hotel, and everyone talked at once as Doaa was pulled into the center of the room for a traditional dance.

Soon, an announcement was made that Bassem was about to enter. In accordance with custom, all the women but Doaa covered their heads. Bassem, clean shaven and dressed in an elegant dark suit, moved toward her. It was the first time he had seen her unveiled. "Is that the same Doaa?" He beamed. "You look amazing, though I think you're even prettier without makeup!" He pulled out a small box from his pocket and took out the gold earrings he had bought for her and clipped them to her ears. The women joined the men in the living room at the buffet and the party began. After eating, the guests danced into the night to a mix of Arabic pop music. It was a rare joyous occasion to remember for everyone there.

A week after the celebrations, as Doaa was going to bed, she reached under her pillow for her engagement ring. She kept it there for safekeeping and only wore it when she went out. To her horror, she felt nothing. She swept her hands frantically over the sheets and lifted the pillow. Her engagement ring was gone! *I don't have any luck in my life!* she thought as she called for her sisters to help her search for it. The family had had guests that evening, friends of the girls'. She couldn't help but wonder if one of them had stolen it. She called Bassem in tears, worried he would think she was careless. "Don't worry," he consoled her. "It's not important. I'll buy you a new one."

A dark thought flashed through Doaa's mind as he spoke: *What if this means we're never going to have a real wedding?* She tried to push the thought from her mind.

Bassem now had a standing invitation to the Al Zamel home. Doaa's sisters adored him, and to Shokri, he was like a son who supported the family and loved his daughter. He always took Bassem's side when he and Doaa quarreled, scolding Doaa, "You must treat your future husband well!" Meanwhile, Doaa was struck with emotions that she'd never before experienced. Hours before Bassem arrived to visit, she would agonize over what to wear, and when his text messages chimed on her phone, she would feel a flutter in her heart. She began to have visions of him meeting other women and discovered the irrational sensation of jealousy. "Don't be silly, Dodo, you are the only woman I have ever and will ever love," he assured her.

The weight of responsibility that she once felt for keeping the family afloat was now shared with Bassem. She realized what a good feeling it was to be supported and protected.

To make more money, Bassem started working in a coal factory. He worked long shifts that started at 7:00 a.m. and ended at 8:00 or 9:00 p.m. The pay was 500 to 600 LE per month, just a bit more than Doaa's wage from her sewing and ironing, which she still did from time to time. After a late shift, he would arrive at Doaa's place exhausted. He was losing weight and coughing from all the dust. Doaa would fix Bassem a plate, and after he was done eating, they would move to the balcony to smoke a *shisha* pipe together until well after midnight. In the later hours of the evening, their talk would eventually turn to their future. They agreed to delay having children until they could finish their educations and find good jobs.

At times, Bassem would tell Doaa that he couldn't see

any future for them in Egypt. One evening, while drinking tea, he told her that since Egypt's military coup he was often taunted by Egyptians. "What are you doing here?" they asked him. "Why don't you go and fight in Syria?" He mostly said nothing when he heard this, but he was starting to think they were right. Doaa reminded him that he came to Egypt because he had been arrested in Syria: "You told me you were tortured in that jail and left for days without food or water."

Every time he received news from Syria, it seemed as if it were always about the death of another one of his friends. Sometimes Doaa was with him when the news came in over the phone. Whenever this happened, Doaa would squeeze his hand in hers and lean her head into the cove of his neck as his tears fell.

To cheer him up, they would listen to their favorite songs from Syria. Placing one earphone in his ear and the other in her own, she would lean her head close to his and they would listen together. They both loved a popular song by the Lebanese pop star Carole Samaha called "Wahshani Baladi," or "I Miss My Country." When the refrain came, they would sing it out loud together:

Oh, God, oh, my dear country, how I miss my
    country . . .
I can't find anything to take the place of what is gone,
    except a moment in the arms of my beloved . . .
Tomorrow I will return, and we will both go back to
    that place . . . and the days will be so sweet.

One weekend, when Bassem took Doaa for a walk on the beach, Doaa knelt down in the sand and with her fingers wrote *Bassem,* to which Bassem added + *Doaa,* then Doaa wrote *Syria* in bigger letters underneath.

Staring at their work, Bassem said suddenly, "Let's go back to Syria. I miss my family. Our place is there."

"There is no way I am going back," Doaa replied, even though only months before she'd wanted to do just that. "I'm responsible for my family and I can't just leave them." She thought of Bassem's returning to Syria and being killed in the war and never seeing him again. "If you go, it will be the end of our relationship," she said, masking her fear for him with anger. "You can take back all the gold that you bought me and go alone," she said defiantly.

"But we have no future here," Bassem insisted, dragging his toe over their names in the sand.

"I could be attacked there and raped in front of you and you would be helpless and unable to defend me," she shouted. "Besides," she said, softening her voice, "there is no work for you in Syria."

Bassem stood in silence for a moment, thinking about what Doaa had said. Then he finally admitted, "You're right."

Doaa took his hand. "Be patient, my love. If you keep looking, you'll find better work in Egypt," she said, trying to make her voice sound as if she believed it herself.

However, the new climate in Egypt was not making things easier for them. One day, as Doaa and Bassem were out for a walk, they got briefly separated as they made their way down the street. A motorbike approached and slowed to a halt beside her. The driver, a nineteen-year-old boy whom she recognized from the neighborhood, suddenly grabbed her arm and pulled her toward him. Doaa instinctively elbowed him, shaking her arm free, but when the boy grabbed at her again, she realized that he intended to force her onto the bike.

Doaa got away from him and ran toward Bassem, yelling, "Bassem, quick! We have to go home now."

Somehow, Bassem had missed the entire episode, but sensing Doaa's fear, he asked, "Did he do something to you?"

Doaa, seeing Bassem's face turn red with anger, decided that it would be best if they left before the situation escalated. "No," she lied. "Nothing happened."

"That's not true, he did something, didn't he?"

Before she could respond, Bassem strode up to the young Egyptian biker and punched him in the face. The bike fell to the ground and the man leaped at Bassem. The two men began to fight, throwing punches and trying to wrestle each other to the ground.

"Bassem, stop, please, for God's sake, stop," Doaa yelled, worried that Bassem would get hurt and that the fight would only attract attention and get them into trouble.

"Go home, Doaa, I'll catch up with you," he yelled as he turned toward her.

The motorcyclist, seeing that Bassem was distracted, jumped back on his bike and sped away.

Doaa and Bassem collected themselves and headed toward home, but on their way back they saw the bike returning. This

time the biker had a friend with him on the back of the motor-
cycle, and two other men followed on a second motorbike. They
were carrying wooden sticks and shaking them menacingly in
the air. One man drew a knife from his pocket as they closed
in on Bassem and Doaa. Bassem pushed Doaa behind him
and shouted at them to leave her alone.

"You came to ruin us! You are feeding off us," the man with
the knife shouted at them. Doaa yelled for help and began
crying. She took out her phone to call her mother. The family
had moved back into the hotel that had given them refuge
when they first arrived in Egypt. They were again staying
there rent-free since the temperature was dropping and vacationers were beginning to leave the area, and it was just a block
from where Bassem and Doaa were now being surrounded as
the men got off their motorbikes and closed in on them. Hanaa
answered the phone and, as soon as she understood what was
happening, alerted the hotel manager, Khalid, who had been
so kind to the family. Khalid rushed outside and stood between Doaa and Bassem and the men, telling them to leave.
Khalid was well respected in the community, and the men finally turned on their heels, mounted their motorcycles, and
sped away.

Khalid, Bassem, and Doaa returned to the hotel, and Khalid insisted that they go directly to the police station to report
the incident. "If you don't say anything, they could come back
and do worse," he warned. While Khalid tried to convince
them to file a report, the young man who had grabbed Doaa
and his father appeared in the hotel. The father was apologiz-

ing profusely. He acknowledged that his son was deeply troubled and told them, "If he ever does that again, you have every right to report him." Then he turned angrily to his son and ordered, "Get down and kiss Doaa's and Bassem's feet." But his son refused and started to cry. Doaa and Bassem felt pity for the crying troubled boy and decided not to report the incident. They just wanted to move on and stay under the radar of the authorities.

As she lay awake that night, Doaa replayed the scene in her head and realized how close she had again come to being kidnapped. She was grateful to Bassem and Khalid for fending off the men, but she no longer felt safe in Egypt, even with Bassem at her side. The stress of the unpleasant encounter also strained her relationship with Bassem.

One day, after a particularly bitter fight with him, Doaa announced that she wanted to break up, leaving him in shock. The next day Bassem showed up at the house looking ill. His tone serious, he told her, "Doaa, we need to talk. I have decided to go back to Syria. I stayed here for you, and I've accepted a lot of humiliation and hardship in Egypt because of you. And if you don't want to be with me, then there's no reason for me to stay here. I've decided that if you don't want to come with me, then you are free. We can end our engagement."

Hearing this, Doaa cried out, "You can't go! You'll be killed!" But Bassem remained firm. Distraught, Doaa ran out of the apartment, realizing the mistake she had made in breaking up with him. She would be complicit in his death if he left and went back to Syria. Doaa knew that Bassem was struggling with the sadness of recently losing his brother, who had died fighting for the FSA, and that Bassem was plagued with guilt for not having been by his side. Doaa didn't really want Bassem to leave her or to break off their engagement. She'd just been worn down by the stress and hardship of her life in Egypt and had snapped during their fight. Bassem followed her outside and found her sobbing. She begged him to change his mind. He studied her face and shook his head, taking out a tissue to gently wipe away her tears. "I didn't mean it!" she sobbed. "I don't want to break up." Seeing Doaa's distress and realizing that she meant what she said, Bassem took her in his arms and promised never to leave her. He vowed that they would only return to Syria together, when the war ended. From then on, Doaa prayed every night that they would always be together.

That fall, Saja, Nawara, and Hamudi started attending school, while Doaa went back to work. Saja's secondary school was in another part of town and she had to walk a good distance on her own to get there. Almost daily, young men would stand outside the school gates taunting her with insults as she entered.

One day as Saja walked home from school, she noticed a tuk-tuk following her. Two rough-looking local men, with tattoos covering their arms, were inside. "Stop, Syrian girl!" they called out to her. "We like Syrian women and we want to see if you like us as well." Saja kept her head down and continued walking to the primary-school gates where Nawara and Hamudi would be waiting. Upon arriving, she immediately took her siblings with her to the administration office to call her parents to pick them up. Hanaa was in tears when she arrived with two Syrian neighbors for protection. Later that day when Shokri heard about the encounter, he was frantic at the thought that his girls might now be in danger in Egypt.

Hamudi was having a hard time as well. While he loved studying and was a good student, once the Morsi government was ousted and the atmosphere changed, the Egyptian kids who used to be Hamudi's friends started to bully him.

Then one day Hamudi's school announced that they would no longer admit Syrian children. Their parents protested, reminding the school officials that the war in Syria had driven them here and that all they wanted was an education for their kids. They also argued that it went against state policy to deny refugee children an education, and that the teachers had no right to decide this policy. A compromise was reached and the school allowed Syrian students to continue to attend the school, but they were no longer allowed to sit at desks and had to sit on the floor.

Around that time, a menacing-looking man on a moped pulled up in the square outside the hotel where Doaa's family was staying and began shouting. Doaa and her family rushed to their balcony to see what he was yelling about. At the top of his lungs, he shouted, "If any of you parents send your children to our schools, they will be returned back to you cut into pieces." He shouted this threat over and over for all to hear. The Syrian men of the neighborhood who witnessed the scene tried to chase him down, but he sped away before they could get his license plate number to report him. The feeling of fear that Doaa's family thought they had left behind in Syria started to creep back in. Many of their neighbors decided to keep their kids at home from then on, and Shokri and Hanaa took their children out of school as well. Hamudi was devastated and spent his days sulking at home.

Meanwhile, Shokri was struggling to make ends meet with only a few loyal customers, and Bassem could see how badly he was doing, so he offered to partner with him in his salon, and Shokri gratefully accepted. By then Bassem had quite a number of young patrons, and this helped to revive Shokri's business. While the extra income helped the family out some, Bassem knew that he wanted more for himself and his future bride. Even with both of them working long hours, they had no hope of a life of anything other than grinding poverty. They couldn't start a family under these conditions, and Bassem was losing more hope every day that they would ever return to Syria. It felt as if they were wasting their lives in Egypt among a population who didn't seem to want them there. He couldn't be with Doaa as much as he wanted since he worked so much, and he worried that one day he would not be there to protect her when she needed him. Bassem knew that something had to change.

SEVEN

Deal with the Devil

On a balmy June afternoon in 2014, nine months after Doaa and Bassem's engagement, the Al Zamel family was finishing up lunch. Doaa was still living at home with her family since she and Bassem could only move in together after they had a formal wedding.

After helping to clear the plates, Bassem suggested that they all go for a walk before he and Shokri returned to work at the barbershop. The young couple walked ahead of the rest of the family, holding hands and chatting. When they reached the Corniche, Bassem turned to Doaa, his voice lower than usual. He spoke deliberately, as if he had rehearsed what he was going to say. "I have something important to discuss with you. I want us to go to Europe. We have no future here. We're stuck, and we can't go back to Syria." He looked down into her astonished face and began speaking more quickly. "Everyone is going. A friend of mine went to Germany and has applied to bring his family there. It's much better there, Doaa. You could go to school and I can open a barbershop. We can have a home together and start a family." He watched her face hopefully, searching for some sign of agreement. "What do you think? We just need to get the money to go."

All Doaa could think of was the vast sea that stood between Egypt and Europe, and of water closing in over her head and filling her lungs. She still hadn't learned to swim, and just the thought of crossing that expanse of water made her panic. She knew that refugees had no legal way to get to Europe. They wouldn't be able to get the documents they needed to sail on another big ferry, like the one they had taken to Egypt. If they applied for a visa, it would be rejected, and to ask for asylum in Europe, you had to arrive there physically, and Doaa knew that the only way to get there was considered illegal by Egyptian authorities and unsafe by everyone. "Do you mean by a smuggler's boat?" she asked. "Don't even think about it. I won't do it." She knew those boats were small, decrepit, and overcrowded and had heard stories of boats sinking and refugees drowning. She couldn't believe that Bassem would want to risk it. How could she cross the sea in one of those when she couldn't even set foot in water?

"But," Bassem stammered, "you will only be in the water up to your knees, then you'll be safe on the boat. We'll be rescued once we get close to Italy, then we can make our way to Sweden!" Bassem explained how distress signals are sent out as soon as refugee boats reach Italian waters, and that the

Italian coast guard sends ships out to bring everyone safely ashore.

"Absolutely not." Doaa shivered. "My answer is no, Bassem."

But he continued to bring up the subject every chance he got, trying to find a way to convince her. Doaa couldn't understand why he kept insisting when he knew how scared she was of water. Every time they went to the beach together with her family, he saw her keep far from the shore, watching everyone else splash around in the waves. Bassem was a good swimmer, for a reason. He'd told Doaa that back in Daraa when he was about thirteen, he visited a lake with two of his friends. None of them knew how to swim, but they waded in anyway, playfully splashing one another. Then one of his friends moved into deeper water and began gasping for air and flailing his arms. Bassem and his other friend thought their friend was joking, but when they finally reached him, his face was submerged and his body was still. He had drowned. After that day, Bassem had vowed that he would teach himself to swim. "I promised myself that I would never stand by helplessly again while someone I care about drowns," he had told Doaa.

He also told her another story. A few years later he was at a lake with some friends sitting on the rocky shore. By that time, he was a confident swimmer. In the distance, he witnessed a rowboat capsize and a teenage girl fall into the water, obviously in distress. He ran toward the boat and jumped in the water. When he reached the girl, he wrapped her in his arms and pulled her to the shore, possibly saving her life.

However, these stories didn't reassure Doaa. Every time she

imagined being submerged in water with no shore in sight, she thought she would be sick. "Bassem, I don't want gold or expensive furniture and a life abroad in Europe," she told him one night when he was trying, yet again, to convince her. They were alone on the balcony of Doaa's apartment watching the sky darken while the rest of the family was inside listening to the radio. She couldn't imagine a life without them nearby. "I want to stay close to our family. What if we went to Saudi Arabia instead? You used to work there." In Saudi Arabia, they could have a new start and still be close enough to her family, and she wouldn't have to get in a boat to get there.

"You wouldn't like it," he countered. "It's too conservative. You would have to wear a burka. You'd be covered in black from head to toe with only a mesh slit in the material to look through. You won't even be able to go out unless you're with me." Exasperated, he said, "Half of my friends have gone to Europe! I get messages from them on Facebook from Sweden and Germany all the time. They have good jobs and they're going to school. They say we'd be welcome there—not like here." Bassem waited for Doaa to ponder this information, then added, "The other messages I get all the time are from friends back in Syria telling me who has died. Have you forgotten what it was like to see people die every day?"

"Have you forgotten all the horror stories about those boats?" Doaa shot back. "And the stories about refugees like us drowning?" Angered, she stood up quickly and went inside to be with her family, leaving Bassem alone on the balcony. She turned her back on him so that he couldn't see the tears of sadness and frustration spilling down her cheeks.

This went on for two months. Bassem brought it up every chance he had, trying different ways to convince her. "Doaa, you look tired! You're not thriving here! In Europe, your health would improve." Doaa's health was, indeed, worsening every week. Anytime Bassem saw her waver, he reminded her of Europe. "In Europe, you can study. We can open a salon together and you will earn money and finally be able to afford new clothes. You can even have a nice house there. We'll be respected instead of despised and our kids can have a nice life." He showed her pictures that he'd received of his friends smiling in front of historical monuments and blooming parks. One friend was pictured in Amsterdam, standing on a bridge over a canal with the pretty cityscape in the background. Seeing these photos, Doaa couldn't help but listen and dream. Europe seemed like a place of order and hope, a fantasyland of possibility.

The life the photos depicted was so different from the poverty, struggle, and danger she had come to accept as normal. Egypt had nothing for her and her family other than hostility and grueling work at low wages that could never quite provide what the family needed. They barely had enough for food and rent, and anytime they needed anything extra, such as medicine or a pair of shoes for Hamudi when he outgrew his, they had to borrow money that they couldn't repay or sell one of their few remaining treasures. Doaa had no way to finish high school in Egypt, and she had all but given up on her dream of going to university. Like thousands of other Syrian refugees, she felt stuck in a life of limbo in a country where its own citizens were facing a sinking economy, high inflation, and rising food prices. In Egypt, Syrian refugees were tolerated, but with few possibilities to find real work and fully integrate into society.

Doaa began to wonder what it might be like to walk out the door without the fear of being abducted, and for her siblings to go to school without the fear of being harassed, beaten up, or worse. She remembered what it was like when her mother wasn't always sick and her father wasn't always exhausted, and when Hamudi was a cheerful little boy with a chance at a normal childhood. None of that was possible now in Egypt.

And in Syria, things were only getting worse. Hundreds of people died in a chemical weapons attack in Damascus that the Assad government was accused by the international community of carrying out. Extremist jihadists now came under the umbrella of rebel groups and they began fighting each other, weakening what moderate FSA opposition there was. In particular, a rising and violent organization called the Islamic State was gaining territory and imposing its fundamentalist doctrine and severe interpretation of sharia, Islamic law, on Syria. At least one-third of the population was now uprooted, with 3 million of them struggling as refugees in the neighboring countries of Lebanon, Jordan, Turkey, and Egypt.

Doaa slowly began to consider the possibility of leaving. However, Bassem began wavering in his decision to move on.

He loved Doaa too much to force her to do something that ter-rified her and began to have second thoughts. He decided that he should go to Europe on his own and then, once he was set-tled, send for Doaa and her family. He had heard of programs in Europe that reunited refugees with family members who had stayed behind. All you had to do, his friends had told him, was get there and ask for asylum, then apply to bring your family into the country as well. They would then be issued visas and plane tickets.

"You could join me in no time," he told Doaa when he re-layed his revised plan to her. They were sitting side by side at a small table in their favorite café, sipping tea and smoking a *shisha* pipe while Bassem took a break from work.

Doaa, stunned, set down her cup. "I won't let you go alone," she said without hesitation. "I can't be separated from you!"

"You're just jealous," Bassem teased her. "You think that if I go to Europe ahead of you, I'll find a beautiful European woman to replace you."

Doaa punched him in the shoulder. "Fine," she shot back, "you go find one, and I'll find an Egyptian husband." While they joked about this, deep down Doaa was hurt that Bassem would consider going to Europe without her, and maybe she was a little afraid that he might actually find a glamorous woman in Europe that he liked better than her.

"I'm just kidding, Dodo. I would never look for anyone else. You are the only one for me. Finding someone else would be like trying to replace the moon with the stars."

Still unsettled, Doaa rested her head on his shoulder. "You

can't ever go anywhere without me." She felt her head rise and fall with his breath. But she could tell that Bassem was set on going, with or without her. She was tired of seeing him struggle in Egypt and knew she had no good case to convince him to stay. She felt that if she refused to let him go, she would be standing in the way of his future, yet she couldn't stand the idea of staying behind if he left. Her life was with him, one way or another, and neither of them had a life in Egypt. She began to think that perhaps she could brave the water if it meant having a shot at a decent life with the man she loved. She told herself that she would also be helping her family— sending money to them and eventually bringing them to a better place.

What she didn't know was that Bassem had already begun discussing his idea with her mother. "It's up to you," Hanaa told the young man she loved like a son, "but I think you should break up with Doaa before leaving."

"Never!" he exclaimed, stung by the idea of it. "I'm going because I want to give Doaa everything she wants." He continued to plead his case, and Hanaa finally gave in and told him that if he was dead set on going, it was fine with her, but she felt that he should travel ahead, find a place for the family, and then apply for Doaa to join him later as his wife. "I do not want her traveling with those smugglers," Hanaa said. "Anyway, there's no way she'll ever set foot in the water."

A few days later, Doaa told her mother that she had decided to go to Europe with Bassem. Hanaa was devastated at the thought of Doaa's making the difficult, dangerous journey, but understood that they felt this was their only shot at a better life. But just thinking about Doaa's being crammed on a boat with hundreds of other refugees horrified Hanaa. However, she knew that Doaa, having made her decision, would be adamant about carrying it out. "Either you let me go to Europe, or you can send me back to Syria," Doaa told her mother the first time Hanaa protested. She looked at her determined daughter, now nineteen years old and an engaged woman, and knew that she couldn't stop her.

That year already, over two thousand refugees and migrants had lost their lives attempting to sail to Europe, and it was only the beginning of August. Late summer and early fall, when the seas were relatively calm and the weather warm, was peak season for refugees to sail across the Mediterranean. More lives would inevitably be lost at sea. Worldwide wars, conflict, and persecution had forced more people to flee their homes and seek refuge and safety elsewhere than at any other time since people began keeping track of the displacements. By the end of 2014, UNHCR would record close to 60 million forcibly displaced people, 8 million more than in the previous year. Half of those were children. Every day that year, on average, 42,500 people became refugees, asylum seekers, or internally displaced, a fourfold increase in just four years.

The chief reason for the massive increase in refugees was the war in Syria. With refugee populations swelling into the millions in neighboring countries, and with little opportunity to work and educate their children, more and more people were risking their lives on dangerous journeys to reach a better life in Europe. People fleeing directly from the relentless violence in Syria found criminal agents in their home cities who not only offered to smuggle them across the border, but, for the right price, across the sea to the promised land they would supposedly find in Europe.

The lucrative business of smuggling people away from the wars and poverty of Africa had quickly expanded from Libya to meet the growing demand from Syrians and Palestinians for a sea route from Egypt.

The smugglers were not difficult to find through word of mouth in refugee neighborhoods or on Facebook, where they advertised what looked like vacation packages on luxury yachts. Two tickets to Europe would cost Bassem and Doaa $5,000, with $2,500 to be paid up front, and the rest being paid if they made it safely to Italy. The smuggler Bassem found was a Syrian middleman using a fake name who was known in the community as the go-to front man. He told Bassem that he could sell him passage on a safe ocean liner and that the journey would take no longer than a few days.

As the day to leave approached, Doaa began to have a sense of foreboding about the trip. One day as she and Bassem were at their favorite café, talking about the smugglers' promises of safe passage, she shared her fears with him. She told him she'd had a premonition that the boat would sink.

"You worry too much, Dodo," Bassem admonished her. "I have just as strong a feeling that it will be fine." But he wouldn't tell her about his own dark fears. Bassem always wanted to be strong for her, and that meant keeping his concerns to himself.

Bassem didn't have enough money left in his savings to pay for the trip, and the Al Zamel family had no extra cash at all. To come up with the money, Doaa sold the gold bracelets and necklace Bassem had bought her for their engagement, and the laptop he had given her as a gift. Hanaa also sold some of her jewelry to pitch in, reluctant to see the pieces go, but wanting to invest in her daughter's future and willing to pay extra for a safe boat. Bassem's family in Syria also wired him $200 to help out, and all this added up to $2,500, enough for the down payment plus 500 euros to start up in Europe. They had no idea how they would come up with the rest, but figured that once they were there, they could borrow and work to pay off their debt. Bassem paid the smuggler and was told to wait for a call.

On August 15, 2014, that call came. Doaa packed one small black duffel bag with her most precious belongings—her Quran; a new gold-colored top and trousers that Bassem had bought her; the remaining engagement jewelry; a silver set with a bracelet, necklace, and a ring with fake diamonds; and a Syrian metal jewelry box decorated with hearts. She said a tearful good-bye to her father, who had to stay behind to work, holding him close and breathing in his familiar scent of shaving cream and the *shisha* pipes he loved. Then she stepped into a taxi with Bassem, her mother, and her siblings. Hanaa insisted that she and the children accompany Doaa and Bassem to see them off.

Bassem gave the driver the address the smuggler had texted him of an apartment in the coastal resort town of Al Agami, about twelve miles west of Alexandria.

When Doaa and Bassem entered the two-room apartment in one of the high-rises along the El Nakhil Beach, they found it filthy and hot. Flies darted from one corner to the next above the few pieces of furniture, which were covered in dust, and appliances that were caked in a heavy rust. Two other Syrian families had arrived before them, sitting in the gloomy room on the sofa or on the floor with their restless children. Including Bassem and Doaa, there were thirteen of them in total. Meanwhile, Hanaa and her children had settled nearby in another shabby apartment owned by the smugglers while they waited for Bassem and Doaa to take off. Bassem called the smuggler to ask when they would leave. The smuggler instructed him to be patient and to stay on call, that it could be at any time depending on the weather and how easily they could get around the police. After several hours went by, Bassem called the smuggler back. He never told Doaa much of what was said during these exchanges, but he conveyed that they would be leaving soon.

They left the apartment for a brief spell to get some fresh air and to buy falafel sandwiches from a beachside stand. Doaa felt self-conscious from the stares that the locals were giving her. She and Bassem and her family were obviously not there for a vacation, and everyone knew that the Syrians in the area were trying to leave the country. They never received a phone call from the smuggler that day or the next, and soon the days and nights started to blend together for Doaa. Everyone was jumpy and anxious.

Finally, Bassem's phone rang one evening in the apartment. "Get ready," the voice on the other end said brusquely. "Leave the apartment in a half an hour, at 9:00 p.m. Go downstairs and don't draw any attention to yourselves. The bus will be waiting in the street behind the building." The smuggler warned Bassem to pack light, that there would be no room for luggage. Doaa added a bag of dates and two bottles of water to her duffel bag, then carefully wrapped their passports in plastic wrap, which she then placed in a sandwich bag, and zipped everything in a side pouch of the duffel bag along with their wallet bulging with five one-hundred euro bills and two hundred Egyptian pounds. Around her, the other refugees gathered their own belongings.

They all left the apartment with their bags, and Doaa and Bassem met with Doaa's family to say their good-byes. They hugged Hanaa, Saja, Nawara, and Hamudi as Doaa's eyes overflowed with tears. She could barely speak through her sobs. She worried that this could be the last time she would ever see them.

"Please look after yourselves. Call when you arrive. We will be worrying about you every minute," Hanaa told them as the situation suddenly became more real to her. "Are you sure you don't want to change your minds? Bassem, you can come live with us. Please don't go!" Hanaa had been trying to be brave for Doaa, but was now overcome with fear for her daughter and future son-in-law.

Doaa tried to reason with her. "Mom, nothing will change here." Doaa fought to control her tears and steady her voice with determination. "It is never going to get any better. We have made up our minds," she said resolutely.

Then, nine-year-old Hamudi turned to Bassem and demanded with his hands on his hips, "Why don't you go by yourself and leave Doaa here? I'm going to miss her."

Doaa smiled and hugged Hamudi again. "Don't worry, once I get to Europe, I'll bring you there, too, and we will be all together and things will be much better."

Finally, in the dark, Doaa and Bassem turned and walked away from Doaa's family toward a dim street corner where the two other Syrian families were waiting. After some time a small white bus pulled up, and a large, barbaric-looking man, who was unshaven and dressed in all black, stepped out and ordered them to board, joining about thirty other people already on the bus, seated on top of each other to fit in. No kindness or welcome was in his voice. Doaa sat on Bassem's lap and rested her arms on the duffel bag. No one on the bus spoke, but they nodded to the newcomers in solidarity.

As the bus took off, Doaa whispered to Bassem under her breath, "These smugglers are thugs, Bassem. I don't trust them and they frighten me." Bassem tried to reassure her that it would all be okay, even though this was not what the smuggler who had sold them the journey had promised.

One of the smugglers made his way down the aisle. He was

smaller than the man who had told them to board, but he was also dressed head to toe in black and spoke just as harshly. Noticing Doaa, he barked at her, "What do you have in your bag?"

"Just some clothes and dates and water, as we were told," Doaa replied timidly.

He nodded. "Keep your passport with you at all times, and hide it in your clothes." Then he moved on and repeated the same question and command to the next row.

After what seemed like an hour, the minibus came to a halt and they were ordered to get off. The group was immediately herded into the back of a large truck meant for transporting sand. While it was dark outside, it was pitch-black in the container once the smugglers closed the back hatch, sealing them in. Everyone was crammed together with no room to move, no windows, and no air circulation. The children were strangely quiet, and Doaa noticed that one woman was visibly pregnant. "These thugs are inhuman," Doaa whispered under her breath. "I don't have a good feeling about this."

Doaa and Bassem could tell from the noise of honking horns, music, and voices that the truck was traveling through populated areas, but after a while the only sound was of the wheels bumping up against potholes and stones. Doaa held Bassem's hand as she peered through the darkness at her fellow refugees, wondering what circumstances had driven each of them to embark on this dangerous journey. After an hour, the truck halted abruptly, and the back hatch opened. Doaa gratefully gulped the fresh air. She was stiff from sitting squeezed up against the other people, and her legs shook as she jumped down from the truck and discovered that they had arrived at a barren coast. Other refugees had arrived before them, clustered in groups of families or friends, sitting in the sand and waiting silently in the dark.

Including the forty other passengers from Doaa and Bassem's truck, they estimated that about two hundred people were gathered on the beach, now at the mercy of their ten criminal travel agents. The smugglers were all barefoot and dressed in black with their pant legs rolled up to their knees. They told the refugees to remain completely silent and explained that they were doing everything they could to evade the police and the coast guard, but by many accounts, they were also paying off officials to turn a blind eye to the smuggling. Doaa checked her watch. It was 11:00 p.m.

The wait in silence was excruciating. It was cold and she wished that she had worn a sweater under her thin jacket.

After two hours, the smugglers divided the refugees on the beach into three smaller groups without explanation. One hundred people were in the first group, with the second and third groups having fifty each. Doaa and Bassem were in the first group. As soon as it was formed, they heard a smuggler shout, "Run!" Bassem picked up their bag and together they set off in the black night toward the sound of the breaking waves. It was cloudy and thus dark and difficult to see. Doaa couldn't even see her hands as they swung in front of her as she took her steps. After a few minutes, a voice ordered them to stop running, keep quiet, then to start again. They could hear the sound of waves crashing and the heavy breathing of their fellow travelers, but they had no sense of orientation except from the smugglers who led them. Their eyes had adjusted to the darkness, but no boat was in sight.

Instead, as they were making their way to the shore, they stumbled into a group of uniformed coastguardsmen asleep on the beach. At the sight of them, the entire group turned on their heels and ran in the opposite direction. Doaa and Bassem were running at the head of the crowd when they heard the sound of bullets and shouts of "You *kilaab* [dogs]! Stop!" Running faster, they shouted to the other refugees, warning them, "It's a trap! Run!"

Bassem took Doaa's hand as they sprinted. Their black bag was strapped to his back, weighing him down. Doaa tried to get him to abandon it, telling him that nothing in it was worth getting shot over. "No," he insisted, "it has all our memories inside." Then suddenly he tripped and fell. The coastguardsmen were gaining ground behind them. Doaa pulled him up and they kept running. The group that ran with them was getting smaller. The families with children and the elderly had surrendered, unable to outpace the guards. A girl Doaa's age was running alongside Doaa and Bassem. She had lost track of her family and wanted to stop, but Doaa took her hand, telling her, "Stay with us. We'll help you."

When they finally reached the main road, Doaa checked

her watch again. It was 3:00 a.m.—they had been running for almost two hours. No houses were along this stretch of road, only empty desert, and soon other Syrians from their group who had escaped joined them. One was speaking in a loud voice into his phone to one of the smugglers, demanding that they come and pick them up. After the call ended, a barrage of questions ensued. Where were they? Did the smugglers set the trap intentionally, knowing that the coastguardsmen would be there? "There are always arrests," one man said knowingly. "It allows the coast guard to show they're doing their job. They get their cut from the smugglers for allowing part of the group to make it to the boat."

So that's why they divided us into groups, Doaa thought angrily.

Bassem, Doaa, and the girl they were helping walked over to the nearby road. Doaa could see a cluster of farms ahead of them. As she and Bassem made their way toward the farms, Doaa looked back to see that the girl had stayed behind with another group of Syrians.

As they continued forward, Doaa saw a gang of over twenty menacing-looking young men carrying sticks and knives walking toward their group. "I was in touch with your organizers," one of them said as he approached, trying to sound friendly. "I was told to help you. We'll take you back to the boat." Doaa and Bassem had a bad feeling about the men, but they didn't know what else to do. At a loss for an alternative, they followed the men down a side road.

One of the men looked at him and said harshly, "Don't worry about them!"

"They'll catch up. Keep moving, or the police will find and arrest you," another said.

"Keep close to me," Bassem told Doaa. She was the only girl among the group, and he was afraid the men would kidnap or rape her, and that he wouldn't be able to stop them. Doaa moved in closer to Bassem, feeling as if they'd made a terrible mistake in following these men. Allowing themselves to fall behind the pack, Doaa and Bassem whispered together, coming up with a plan. They stopped walking and Bassem announced, "We want to wait for the others."

The thugs then circled around them, confirming Doaa and Bassem's fears. They demanded that Doaa and Bassem hand over their money and their jackets.

"We have nothing, we gave it all to the smugglers for the journey," Bassem replied. He clutched Doaa's hand and they took off back up to the main road as the thugs gave chase and shouted insults behind them. Doaa and Bassem reached the main road, gasping for breath and hoping that the thugs wouldn't try anything in front of all the cars that were now roaring by. Doaa was crying from exhaustion and fear, and Bassem tried to wave down cars and comfort her at the same time. Doaa stood with him, hoping that a driver would be more sympathetic toward a couple than to a lone man. Her mouth was dry and she felt as if she would faint from a combination of thirst, fear, and despair. "Doaa, watch out!" she suddenly heard Bassem shout. The next thing she knew, he had lunged to her side and pushed her down. Doaa looked up from the ground and saw a truck had veered toward her and would have crushed her had Bassem not yanked her out of harm's way.

Several cars buzzed by, but none stopped to help. Doaa and Bassem were worried that the gang were watching and waiting for them to turn back. Finally, Doaa spotted a police car approaching and was strangely relieved. "Let's give ourselves up, Bassem," she said. "It's better than being attacked by those thugs." Bassem agreed and together they ran out to the street. The police car screeched to a halt beside them. The officers stepped out, guns drawn. First they slammed Bassem against the car to search him as Doaa began to cry again. Then the police asked about the rest of the refugees. "We don't know where they are. We decided to give ourselves up," Doaa lied. They pleaded for water when they got into the backseat of the police car and the officers handed them a bottle to share.

The police drove up and down the area until daybreak looking for others from the group who were attempting to leave the country illegally. At about 6:00 a.m., the police stopped at the place on the beach where the sleeping coastguardsmen had originally spotted the refugees. In the light of dawn, Doaa noticed a small military post that had been hidden in the dark and recognized many of their fellow travelers, including about forty women and several children, sitting on the ground in front of it. The men had their hands tied behind their backs. Doaa and Bassem were taken to join the group. They sat down on the sand with their bag between them. Doaa felt sick and dizzy. She had run for hours without food, water, or rest. She recognized the pregnant woman from the truck when she said, "You look so sick, dear." She handed Doaa a small carton of orange juice with a straw. Doaa sipped the sweet, warm liquid and instantly felt better.

Soon, without explanation, the police began taking everyone's bags. Doaa didn't trust the officer when he said that everything would be returned, and she felt as if a piece of her identity was being taken from her. Around midmorning, when the sun was getting hotter, Doaa grew impatient and went to look for her duffel bag. An officer instructed her to go back to where she was sitting and said he would find it for her. A few minutes later he returned, claiming that he couldn't find it.

Doaa didn't believe him. "Please, it's important to me that I have my things. I don't mind looking myself," she said, rising to confront him. She was tiny against the big-shouldered man. The officer softened and sent three of his men with Doaa to look for her bag. She led them to the place where she had seen the luggage taken and saw only scattered pieces of clothing on the ground. When she spotted her cargo pants crumpled up and trampled on, Doaa returned to the officer and stood before him. "You took my luggage!"

Looking down at her, he said, "How dare you accuse us of stealing!"

But Doaa didn't back down. That bag had held everything that she had. "It was stolen. The things in there are important to me." But it was no use. Everyone's luggage was gone. She thought of her treasured tiny jewelry chest from Syria and her

Quran. Of what value were those things to these officers? She was grateful that she and Bassem had at least kept their passports and their money concealed under their clothes, but some of the others who had their passports and cash stashed in their bags had lost everything.

After an excruciating wait under the desert sun, the group was asked to stand together for a photograph. Then the women and children were directed to climb into the back of an open-top army truck, which took them up to the main road. Doaa was seated in the back next to a woman who said her name was Hoda, who was about four months pregnant. Doaa couldn't imagine making the difficult journey pregnant and said as much to Hoda. "We have no future," Hoda said, her hand resting on her belly. "I'm leaving for the future of the child."

Although there was room in the back of the truck, the men, about fifty of them, including Bassem, were forced as punishment to walk, handcuffed, in the midday heat, for miles up to the main road. When they were finally allowed to board the truck, Bassem came and sat next to Doaa. "Are you okay?" he asked, taking her hand. His lips were dry and cracked. "I didn't realize it was going to be this hard."

The truck started up again and the guards drove them to the Birimbal detention center in the swampy, rural town of Matubus on the outskirts of Alexandria. Doaa and Bassem were separated there, and Doaa had to wait in a line with the other women to have her mug shot taken and to sign a document confessing that she had attempted to leave Egypt illegally. An officer from the national security department asked her questions about the smugglers. What were their names? What did they look like? How much did you pay? Where did you leave from? She answered as best she could, replying that one was called Abu Mohammed.

"Seems to me they are all called Abu Mohammed," the officer joked. Another officer looked at her in concern and said kindly, "Don't go with those smugglers. They're no good." She was told that she and Bassem were sentenced to ten days in prison for trying to leave the country illegally and was taken to a room that was already packed with women and children. Men were kept separately in another location. There was no running water and the toilet didn't flush. The stench and the flies made Doaa feel nauseated and she couldn't eat. Each inmate received a small mat to sleep on but no blanket, and there was nowhere to shower. Doaa had no change of clothes and no way to keep clean, which added to her misery.

As the days wore on, the children developed scabies and their mothers found it hard to stop their children's crying. Female officials from UNHCR visited to interview and check on the prisoners, advocating on their behalf and delivering food, toiletries, blankets, and medical supplies. Doaa was allowed to make one call to her family, and she was able to talk to her mother just long enough to calm her parents' fears and to tell them that she would be released in a few days.

A sympathetic medical officer from Doctors Without Borders

visited and examined Doaa, urging her to eat and warning her to take care of her health. During his rounds in the men's section, he also examined Bassem. He warned Bassem that he, too, was in poor health, pointing to his jutting cheekbones as a sign that his nutrition and food intake were low. But the doctor also noticed that Bassem's spirits were high and asked him about his situation. Bassem told the doctor he was heading to Europe to start a new life with his fiancée, Doaa, who was in the women's section of the prison. He described his plans to go with her to Sweden to open his own barbershop and get married. When he discovered that the doctor had examined Doaa, he probed him about her condition. As soon as the checkup was finished, Bassem rose and approached one of the guards, pleading with him for a visit with his fiancée. The burly policeman refused, but Bassem was persistent. "Just for a few minutes, please!" he begged. Soon the rest of the men chimed in to support him: "Can't you see he's in love?" The guard capitulated and let Bassem visit Doaa for a few minutes. This ritual repeated itself every day until their release, one day short of their ten-day sentence. The young couple became favorites of both the guards and the other prisoners.

When their sentence was up, Bassem, Doaa, and eight other Syrians were driven to Alexandria, where they filled out forms to renew their residency permits and paid a fine. On their bus ride back to Gamasa, Bassem called one of the smugglers. "Why did you report us?" he demanded. The man denied any involvement and asked if they wanted to try again to get to

Europe. He still had their money, he reminded them. Bassem said he would call him back and hung up.

Doaa's family was waiting for her and Bassem when they reached the apartment building. For the first time in ten days, Doaa and Bassem had a shower. Hanaa prepared Doaa's favorite dish, stewed *molokhia* leaves with coriander seeds, garlic, and onion served with steamed rice. Neighbors came to hear about their ordeal and warned them that they shouldn't try to leave again. The authorities were cracking down, they said, and they might not get off as easy a second time.

But now, in August 2014, the Syrian refugee population in Egypt was growing restless. The war had spread to the far reaches of their country, and their hopes of returning to Syria were growing dim. Extremist groups linked to al-Qaeda, and new terrorist organizations such as the al-Nusra Front and the Islamic State, had filled in the gaps where the moderate opposition, who were now outgunned, had failed to take control. There were no longer two sides in the battle for Syria, but a range of players vying for territory and power. Most of those who had risen up in protest back in March 2011 had lost their lives or fled the country. By the fourth year of the war, few of those fighting the regime represented the values of the original resistance movement. Increasingly, opposition groups were battling each other. The more moderate militias such as the Free Syrian Army were fighting not just the government, but the radical extremists of ISIS as well. And on the government's side, foreign fighters from Iran and from Hezbollah, the Shiite

Islamist militant group and political party based in Lebanon, boosted their capacity while starting an international proxy war that would bring in Russia on the government's side, and Saudi Arabia, Qatar, and Turkey on the other. Eventually the United States, France, and the UK would join in the fight against both Assad and ISIS as well. Well-meaning UN-brokered attempts at peace talks would collapse, and pledged cease-fires would continually unravel.

Cities such as Daraa were emptied of their original residents, who left behind their destroyed homes to seek relative safety in other parts of the country, across borders, or increasingly across the Mediterranean Sea. Many of Bassem's friends who had made it to Europe continued to encourage him to do the same. The journey would be difficult for a few days on the sea, but after that things would be fine, they assured him. His friends had crossed the Mediterranean and made it to Germany, Sweden, and Holland, and now they were studying or working there. They told him over Facebook chat that they could learn the language in six months, and once they did that, they could easily find work.

Europe had sympathy for Syrian refugees at that point. The number of Syrians arriving in Europe was increasing, but was still relatively small—fewer than eighty thousand in 2014—and governments recognized that they were fleeing from war, so they quickly waved them through the asylum process.

European governments had always found it more politically expedient to contain refugee populations close to the countries they had fled from, including the 3 million refugees from Syria in its neighboring countries. Funding grew to enable UNHCR and its partners to provide shelter, food, education, health care, and other services for the many desperate refugees in countries such as Egypt. But the millions of euros that came from global governments didn't match the growing needs of a swelling and increasingly needy group of people. Once middle-class, professional Syrians were now living off handouts, and scraping for rent in substandard dwellings, and taking work from employers who exploited them. Desperate for income, many resorted to sending their young children to work instead of school, picking vegetables for as little as $4 a day or selling flowers in the city streets. Meanwhile the refugees grew restless and anxious to move to countries where it was legal for them to work and where their children could go to school.

When Syrians began to land on the shores of Italy in noticeable numbers, European politicians sought the cooperation of origin countries such as Egypt to help stop the boats. Financial incentives were offered for crackdowns on smugglers and detention and fines for refugees who attempted to leave the countries illegally. The message was clear: Stay in your own region. But for Syrians such as Doaa and Bassem, Egypt was suffocating their dreams.

After Bassem and Doaa finished their welcome-home meal, Hanaa begged them not to leave again, but later when they discussed what they should do next, Doaa told Bassem, "It is better to have a quick death in the sea than a slow death in Egypt." Hearing this, Bassem picked up the phone and called the smuggler back.

A couple of days later, they got the call to leave again the next day. This time, they were given the address of a small flat in Alexandria where four families, who had arrived before them, had gathered to await the signal to depart. They boarded a bus that same night. Once again, the bus was packed with families, along with two smugglers who received calls every few minutes and barked orders at the driver, who would then veer off in another direction. "They don't know what they are doing," Doaa whispered to Bassem as she fell against him. The bus sped up and one of the smugglers announced that a police car was behind them. The driver steered the bus off the paved road and onto the dirt track of a big farm, accelerating. Women screamed and children cried as the tires hit potholes and narrowly missed palm trees. The police officers fired shots, hitting the back and sides of the bus. The next thing Doaa and Bassem felt was the impact of the bus crashing into a wall as it abruptly stopped. The police surrounded the bus, ordering the smugglers out first. They put plastic bags over their heads and tied each at the neck, then forced them to take off their clothes except for their underwear. The police tied the smugglers at the ankles and kicked and beat them, creating a show of humiliation for the stunned group of refugees observing the scene.

"You're back, welcome back, dear visitors!" an officer said to Doaa, laughing. She recognized him as the officer who had caught them the first time. Bassem pleaded with him not to take them back to the prison and offered instead to pay him to be released. At first the officer refused, but he later returned with a preposterous offer. For $5,000 he would set them free. Bassem and Doaa realized that they were going back to prison.

First they were taken to a stadium that had been used as army barracks to spend the night, then the next day they were taken back to the same police station as before to sign for a second time documents admitting guilt for attempting to leave the country illegally. They were returning to the same prison as before.

On the second day in prison, Doaa awoke with a terrible headache and nausea. It was now August 28, the first anniversary of Doaa and Bassem's engagement, and Doaa was in despair. How had others made it to Europe and not them? she wondered.

A sharp pain gripped her lower back and was shooting into her sides. She sat in a corner with her knees folded up into her chest. Doaa asked the guards for the doctor, but had to wait in excruciating pain for the regular rounds of the Doctors Without Borders physician, who was due to come in the next day.

When he saw Doaa's condition, the doctor demanded that she be released and admitted to the hospital right away. After several phone calls to his higher-ups, the police officer in charge received permission, and two officers from the detention center drove Doaa and the doctor to the nearest clinic, thirty minutes away. Doaa felt humiliated being accompanied by the police and self-conscious from the stares of the people in the waiting room.

The policemen, all men in their fifties who reminded Doaa

of her father, had grown fond of her and told everyone that she was no criminal. They asked the hospital staff to take her in for tests. A nurse took her into an examination room for an X-ray and helped her take off her clothes. She took one look at Doaa's body and started to cry. "You are so thin!" she said as she guided her to the scale and recorded that Doaa weighed only eighty-eight pounds. Doaa confided in the nurse her story about how she'd ended up in jail. The nurse admitted how she despised Bashar al-Assad but loved the Syrian people. She then placed ten pounds in Doaa's hand for a sandwich and began reciting a prayer from the Quran. Doaa was deeply touched by the nurse's kindness. When the doctor entered the room, the nurse instructed him, "Take care of her as if she were your own daughter." During the examination, the doctor ruled out appendicitis, but he diagnosed Doaa with kidney stones and a stomach infection and decided to keep her in the hospital overnight for observation.

When she returned to the prison the next day, the guards were protective of her, knocking on the door to the women's cell to check whether Doaa had taken her medication. Bassem visited, too, when they would let him, counting her pills and asking the other women to keep an eye on her. After ten days, they were released once more. "Don't try escaping Egypt again," the presiding officer told them, "and good luck."

Doaa again decided that they should make another attempt to leave for Europe. Her experience in prison had been demeaning, but it had changed her perspective. The idea of resuming their life in Egypt seemed intolerable. Bassem was more reluctant to try again, but the smugglers still had their $2,500. So Bassem made the call and was given yet another address in Alexandria. It was the same scenario, but a different apartment. They were greeted by another Syrian family at the house—a husband, wife, and four children, refugees like themselves with the determination to risk their lives for the hope of a future better than the limbo they lived in now.

EIGHT

Ship of Horrors

At 11:00 a.m. on September 6, 2014, the call came. Doaa carefully packed a change of clothes for Bassem and herself, their toothbrushes, a sealed large plastic bag of dates, and a big bottle of water into the Mickey Mouse backpack she'd kept from her school days back in Syria. She carefully wrapped their passports and engagement contract in plastic wrap, then dropped them in a sandwich bag and folded over the end. Next, she wrapped her mobile phone and wallet with the five hundred euros and two hundred Egyptian pounds that they still had from their previous escape attempts in a separate plastic bag and secured each bundle underneath the straps of her red tank top, the first of four layers of clothes she had carefully selected for the journey. The plastic immediately made her skin sweat in the humid late-morning heat.

Five minibuses were waiting outside the apartment complex in Alexandria, already packed with fellow Syrian and Palestinian refugees, who looked up as the doors opened but said nothing. Doaa and Bassem climbed inside and found a single seat in the back for them to share, wedging their bag and their two life jackets between them and the window. People were packed in so tightly that Doaa could barely breathe, and a hushed tension filled the bus as it moved toward the highway as part of a convoy with the other buses. Doaa pulled her jacket up around her face, as if it could shield her from any security forces that might be watching. Just when she felt like she was about to faint from the stifling air inside the bus, they veered off into a truck stop and pulled up alongside a big run-down bus. They were ordered to get off and join other passengers in the bigger bus. People on this second bus were already sitting on each other's laps or standing crammed together. "Get in, dogs!" they heard from inside the bus. "Men on one side, women on the other!" There were more women and children than men, so this rule quickly broke down. Another smuggler rasped, in an uglier tone, "If anyone opens his mouth, we'll throw you out the window!" Of all the smugglers that Doaa and Bassem had dealt with in their previous attempts to leave, these were the roughest and most cruel.

Bassem usually assumed the role of reassuring Doaa, but was instead thinking about a way to get them off the bus. He didn't trust the men in charge at all. He was unsettled by Doaa's words as they sat down: "I feel like we are being taken to our deaths." Just days before, she had also said to him as they were having coffee on the balcony that, as much as she tried, she couldn't picture them in Italy or Sweden or anywhere in

Europe. Everything after they boarded a boat was blank to her, as if the door to a house had opened and nothing was inside but emptiness. "The boat is going to sink," she told Bassem flatly. Bassem had brushed off her remark, joking that her fear of the water was getting the best of her, but now he wondered.

As he was about to raise his doubts to Doaa, the bus turned into a rest stop. For a moment, as they left their seats and were allowed to enter the shop to buy refreshments and to use the toilet, they felt giddy, grateful for the brief respite, even if it was just to buy a snack. But when the signal came for them to board the bus again, with no information about where they were headed or how long it would take, and no trust in their guides, the gamble they were taking with their lives returned to sharp focus. Bassem wanted to stay at the rest stop, but Doaa was afraid that the smugglers, who were hitting and shoving people who were moving too slowly as they reboarded, would hurt them if they tried. So they returned to the bus, their destiny no longer in their own hands.

It was past 9:00 p.m. when the bus set off again. It took them through back roads past abandoned or half-constructed buildings. The smugglers walked the aisles carrying sticks and waving them menacingly, and occasionally smacking anyone whose children cried too loudly or who dared to ask where they were going. Doaa looked out the window and recognized a sign for Khamastashar Mayo—a section of Damietta's beach. "We are close to home!" she said to Bassem. "We came to this beach with our family!" The smugglers had obviously chosen a different departure point from the one near Alexandria and had driven them down the coast toward Doaa's place in Gamasa, which was now just a few kilometers away. Her phone's battery was dead so she asked a man seated close to her if she could use his mobile to call her mother. "We are leaving now! Pray for us. We will call you when we arrive."

"Look after yourself, *hayati,* be careful," Hanaa replied. "May God protect you."

At 11:00 p.m. they came to a halt about half a kilometer from a barren, sandy beach. "Get out and run to the shore!" the smugglers shouted. The passengers filed out and noticed other buses already parked there, and hundreds of people ahead of and behind them. Those ahead of them were wading through the shallow waves. Bassem kicked off his flip-flops, took Doaa's hand, and they sprinted toward the water. He thought they would be safer somehow if they got ahead of the crowd. He led her to the edge of the sea, passing families with children that were slower than them. As they reached the shore, Doaa pleaded with him to wait before stepping into the swell. "I need to gain my courage," she said.

"Trust in God's will, Doaa, and be brave, this is our only chance," he replied, gripping her hand as he charged into the shallow water. Doaa felt the waves swallow her calves, then her knees. It was soon up to her waist, and she feared she would be swept away. She felt as if she were moving through her worst nightmare.

One of two outboard wooden dinghies, painted in light blue and about three and a half meters long, was moving toward them, but to reach it, they had to struggle through breaking waves until the water was up to Bassem's shoulders. It would have been over Doaa's head, but her thin life jacket, along with her tight grip on Bassem, just barely kept her afloat. The vest rose to the surface and circled her face, keeping just her chin above water. She realized that the beach shop that had sold them the vests for $50 apiece had scammed them; these were fakes. A new industry produced life jackets to exploit the refugee trade. Some of the vests' fillings were cheap absorbent material. Or, in Doaa's case it seemed, thin sheets of foam that provided only the slightest buoyancy. She did her best to keep her face above the water and the vest from floating over her head. They reached the dinghy, and Bassem pulled himself over its side while a smuggler lifted Doaa in. People were hauled into the boat until at least twenty people were crowded on board. Everyone was ordered to sit still, shoulder to shoulder, as a man pulled the cord to start the motor to take them to a larger boat waiting on the horizon.

An Egyptian man, obviously another smuggler, stood in the center of the dinghy and demanded, "Hand over your Egyptian money and your phone SIM cards now! You won't have any use for them in Europe." He barked when the people closest to him hesitated. The people in the dinghy had no choice but to hand over their money and phones. Doaa pulled out the wallet from inside her tank top and slipped it down between her knees, where she could discreetly peel off one hundred Egyptian pounds, pass it to Bassem, and conceal the rest of the money again. She kept their mobile phone hidden under the strap of her tank top. When they neared the ship that was to take them across the sea, Doaa felt a chill of panic. She and Bassem had never quite believed that the ship that would take them to Europe would look like the cruise liners that were advertised on some of the smugglers' Facebook pages, or the "four-star ship" their front man had described to them over the phone. But this boat's decrepit state was far below their expectations. Its blue paint was peeling and its rims had turned to rust. The apparatus on board for hauling nets made it clear that the boat was a fishing trawler, not a passenger ship. Still, Doaa thought, relieved, *We finally made it through the first phase of our journey, and once I'm on board, I won't have to get in the water again.*

Hundreds of people were already on the boat when Doaa and Bassem climbed on deck, pushed from below and pulled from above by the passengers. They soon learned that a good number of these weary-looking travelers had already been on the boat for days, drifting at sea and impatiently waiting for Doaa and Bassem's group to join them so they could fill every square inch of the trawler. The more people the smugglers could pack in, the more profit they would make. Bassem estimated at least five hundred refugees were on board when they finally set off. If each passenger had paid $2,500 as they had, the smugglers would be collecting $1 million for this journey. Even more if they charged for the children. At least one hundred kids were on board.

It was already so crammed on their boat that when Doaa looked around, she wondered how the others in the buses behind them would squeeze themselves into the remaining millimeters. Suddenly, she heard someone shout, "Police! Police!"—and then the sound of bullets hitting the side of the boat.

"Heads down!" the smugglers yelled, as the engine roared and the boat sped away. People began to dive for the deck, praying aloud that they wouldn't be shot. Doaa held tight to the edge of the boat as she lowered her head to her knees, terrified that she could be swept over the edge as the boat sped over the choppy waves. Only when they were out of range of the bullets did she dare to lift her head. She peered over the edge and realized that she could no longer see the shore through the darkness.

Doaa was frightened as she gripped the edge of the boat because she and Bassem had been separated. When she had first climbed on board, she had been directed to sit on the floor of the women's section on the covered middle deck, while Bassem had been sent to the top deck, where the men were sitting. Doaa sat sandwiched between two women, knees to her chest, trembling and alone. Families were told to find places on the other side of the boat or belowdecks. The ship smelled of fish, and a nasty stench came from the toilets, making everyone on board feel sick. Several of the people around her were vomiting from the choppy waves and the stench.

The passengers began introducing themselves to each other in desperate whispers, trying to find some sense of community in the midst of their misery and fear. Most of the passengers were Syrians, but twenty-seven Palestinian families had come from Gaza and about twenty-five Africans from Sudan and

Somalia, along with about ten Egyptian minors. Only about half of the passengers had life jackets, and Doaa suspected that many of them were no better than hers. One teenaged boy that Doaa met wore a child's-size life vest that came only about halfway down his chest. She began to pray for everyone's safety.

At dawn on Sunday, after a sleepless night for everyone on board, the boat cut its engine as another fishing trawler approached. The smugglers ordered the refugees to switch boats. Doaa couldn't understand the logic of moving to another boat, but had heard that this was a recurring procedure for such clandestine journeys. Different fishing boats had licenses to operate in different areas of the sea, somehow making the smuggling of human cargo even less conspicuous to patrols. The two trawlers pulled alongside each other and, although they were tied together, kept drifting apart then smacking up against each other again. Doaa struggled to her feet and tried to keep her balance as she jumped from one dilapidated boat to the other, reluctantly taking the hand that a smuggler offered her to pull her onto deck of the second boat as another one pushed her toward him.

This time, passengers were allowed to choose where they wanted to sit. Bassem and Doaa reunited on the new ship, and he led her to a space on the deck where they could lean their backs against the side of the boat. They sat on their life jackets and huddled together. With no space to lie down, Doaa leaned her head on Bassem's shoulder, and his head rested on hers.

Once they set off, the crew, in a pathetic attempt to show benevolence, walked the deck handing out tins of expired and rotten processed meat. Bassem settled for some of the dates that they had brought with them, but Doaa couldn't eat at all. When the ship moved, everything in the toilets shifted as well, stirring up a terrible stench that caught in Doaa's nostrils, making it difficult even to breathe. *Just three more days of this, then we will be rescued by the Italians and this nightmare will be over,* she told herself again and again. When the sea was calm, the seasickness temporarily abated, and passengers pulled out the snacks they had packed—cookies, dried fruit, and small boxes of juice, sharing with each other. For a few brief moments, spirits would rise and people would trade tales of their dreams for the future.

Doaa observed the people around her, wondering what had brought them there. She had always been interested in the situation of the Palestinians and had had a few friends who'd lived in the Palestinian neighborhood in Daraa. She was outraged at the injustice of their lives in Gaza when she watched the news. Now she learned that many refugee families on the boat had fled from the latest Israeli offensive. Others were coming from Syria, once a haven for Palestinians and now a place where the government no longer protected them, and where they were being targeted either for their association with the Assad government or their unwillingness to take up arms on either side. Doaa spotted one family of four seated close by. She and the mother in the family started to chat. They were from the Yarmouk Camp for Palestinians in Damascus, and she and her husband, Imad, were trying their best to comfort their two little girls, Sandra, six, and Masa, eighteen months, who were restless and crying. Doaa asked where they were headed. The mother said their destination was Sweden, where her brother-in-law had traveled a year before with their eldest daughter, Sidra, who was eight. They had thought that if they sent their daughter ahead, chances were better that at least some of the family would survive. The mother asked Doaa to hold little Masa, then got to her feet and asked Doaa to pass Masa up to her so she could take her to the toilet. Doaa squeezed the warm little body close to her chest for just a moment, then handed her up to her mother.

Everyone on this boat must have a sad story to tell, Doaa thought, as she watched Masa and her mother make their way across the deck, but she noticed that few people would mention their past. Their talk was instead focused on the future, getting through the ordeal of these miserable days at sea and starting new lives. As the days stretched forward, a kind of solidarity formed among the passengers. People especially reached out to help the children—entertaining them with stories, offering them sips of water, or peeling open rolls of cookies to offer small treats. There was no sectarian, religious, or ethnic division here, just people trying to help each other get through the day.

Doaa longed for the Quran that she had brought to Egypt with her from Syria, her most precious possession. Since her early teens, she had read from it every evening before bed, and at random times during the day when she needed some comforting words to give her peace of mind. After reading from it, Doaa would slip it back into its hard case, which was embossed with a pink-and-white geometric pattern. Her Quran would have soothed her now, she thought, but her thoughts soon turned to anger as she remembered that it was in the black duffel bag that had been confiscated during her first arrest. She was suddenly overcome with hatred for the smugglers and anger at the police and everyone who tried to profit from the desperation of refugees such as herself.

A few moments later, a smuggler approached their section of the boat with a book in his hand. "Someone has dropped this Quran. Does anybody want it?" He was the first of the smugglers who had spoken to them with any kindness. Bassem was chatting with a Palestinian man next to him named Walid who accepted the book, but then, not wanting to appear selfish, Walid turned to Bassem and Doaa and offered it to them. Doaa whispered to Bassem, "I do really want that Quran." Walid smiled kindly and handed it to her. Taking hold of the small holy book, she felt energy and relief return to her body. Just the feel of the soft leather in her hands comforted her. She kissed the cover and opened the book anxiously, reading the words of God inside, and feeling as if she held an object of protection. As she flipped through the pages, she found small slips of paper with handwritten prayers. When she finished reading them, she closed the book carefully, making sure not to lose the notes, and slipped it under her T-shirt close to her heart.

Sometimes the other women sitting close by would join Doaa when she took the Quran out; they would recite prayers alongside her and ask God to guide the ship safely to Italy. The woman sitting directly to her left struck up a conversation, tell-

ing Doaa about her difficult life in one of the Palestinian refugee camps in Lebanon. She asked Doaa what drove her from
Syria and where she was going. When she learned about Doaa
and Bassem's engagement in Egypt and their plans to seal their
marriage in Europe, the young woman, who called herself Um
Khalil, "mother of Khalil," her two-year-old teething son, was
delighted. "You're a bride!" she exclaimed. "We will make you
a lovely wedding when we get to Europe! We will sing and
dance all night!" Doaa was touched. The other woman seated
beside her, a middle-aged Syrian Palestinian, chimed in, "When
we arrive in Italy, we will buy you the nicest dress and have two
big parties—one for your wedding and one to celebrate that
we have arrived!"

"You are so lucky with Bassem," Um Khalil told Doaa,
catching Bassem's eye and smiling at him. At this, Doaa felt
suddenly possessive and turned toward Bassem, and away from
Um Khalil.

Bassem immediately recognized the insecure expression
of jealousy on Doaa's face. "You should keep chatting with
her, she's nice!" he whispered in Doaa's ear.

"What do you mean by that?" Doaa asked, taken aback. Was
he using her to get close to the other woman? she wondered.

Bassem grinned at her. "Are you jealous?" he teased. Then,
seeing that she was truly distressed, he reassured her, "I only
have eyes for you, my love." Hearing this, Doaa curled up
against him and took his hand in hers. "In just two days, we
will be in Italian waters," he predicted. "Then we'll make our
way to Sweden and be married and have our family." He'd

heard from friends who had made it to Europe that once they got to Italy, the smugglers would send out a distress signal, alerting the coast guard to their location using GPS. Sometimes, the smugglers would get picked up by collaborators before the rescue ship arrived, leaving the refugees without a captain or crew, Bassem explained. If not, they pretended to be refugees themselves to avoid being arrested, getting the passengers to vow to not disclose their identities, then the first chance they got, they would abscond from the group.

None of the passengers on board had any idea where they were. There were no landmarks, just a vast body of water surrounding them. Every now and then, people would test their mobile phones for a signal, but there was none.

That night, the passengers shivered in the cold, their thin layers of clothes soaked from waves that had splashed over the deck. Doaa stirred as she felt Um Khalil's baby boy's small fingers touching her face and pulling on her necklace. Instead of being annoyed that her sleep was disrupted, she found that his touch calmed her.

When the sun rose on their third day, their things slowly dried off, but it became swelteringly hot. Doaa's clothes stuck to her, and the plastic-wrapped documents and phone underneath them felt as if they were melting into her skin. Late that afternoon another boat approached. "Move," the smugglers said, ordering them to switch boats yet again. The passengers complained but did as they were told. They had to switch boats if they wanted to move on to the next leg of the journey. To Doaa's surprise only about 150 passengers disembarked along with Bassem and her, while the other passengers remained on the last boat. One of the smugglers explained that the waves were too high for so many people so they had to split up, and Doaa and Bassem felt resigned to follow the directions of the smugglers. Bassem reasoned optimistically that they might reach Italy faster with a smaller number of passengers on board. Doaa looked around her, confused yet hopeful, and noticed that the two little girls Masa and Sandra, along with their parents, had boarded this boat as well. This was the fourth boat they had been on since they had started their journey and she hoped it would be the last.

On Tuesday morning, September 9, four days into their journey, Doaa and Bassem spotted another fishing boat in the distance, and as they moved closer, they realized that it was the same one they had been on the previous day. Again, without any explanation, the boats came together, and the smugglers ordered the refugees to switch boats yet again. On this windy day, the water was choppy. The smugglers tossed ropes to their collaborators on the bigger vessel. The boats crashed together, and Doaa was reminded of the crack of an explosion back in Daraa and the terror she had felt when she heard the sound.

A line of people formed to move back to the original boat. Children were crying as they were tossed like bags of potatoes into the arms of the burly men on the next boat. When it was Doaa's turn, she slipped after they dropped her on the deck of the new boat, falling and sliding to the other side, bruising her elbows. Bassem helped her up. Then they watched in horror as Walid got his hand stuck between the two boats as he was leaping between them. The waves slammed the sides of the boats together and Walid screamed. When he finally pulled himself onto the deck, his fingers were severed from his hand and blood was gushing in all directions. Passengers rushed to wrap his hand in gauze to stop the bleeding, but his fingers were gone. He sat on the deck, sobbing in pain. Doaa stared in distress, too shocked to move.

The smugglers remained unfazed and continued to bark orders and push the remaining passengers on board. One man tripped and fell face forward into an iron pole, splitting his head open. Doaa's stomach turned as she watched a woman who knew him calmly pull out a needle and thread from her bag and sew the gash shut.

When the passengers were settled and the boat started its engines again, a member of the crew circled the deck with a large bag full of stale pita bread. When he handed a few pieces to Bassem, he looked at Doaa and told her, "You need this to stay strong." Doaa shook her head. "Thank you, but I'm not hungry," she replied flatly. Bassem was furious with her as he took her share of the bread anyway. It was their third day at sea and she had only eaten once, just a few mouthfuls from a can of tuna someone had given her. Walid was nearby, in visible pain, clutching his hand. "I feel like I am going to die, it hurts so much," he told Doaa, shaking. She knelt next to him and read him a few verses from the Quran in the hopes that it would provide him some comfort.

The crew on this boat was kinder than that on the first boat.

Shoukri Al-Assoulli, a Palestinian passenger from Gaza who was on the boat with his wife and two small children, Ritaj and Yaman, learned from chatting with the captain that he was not a smuggler, but was also on his way to Europe in hope of refuge. The captain told Shoukri that he had been in prison for years, and that when he got out, he needed to find a way to support his family. So he and some of his friends made a deal with the smugglers to man the boat in exchange for free passage to Europe, where they wanted to look for work. He begged Shoukri and the others not to turn him and the crew in once they got to Europe. They were just like them, he explained, people who couldn't get by in Egypt and were seeking a better life.

The refugees promised him they would not turn him in, but they were beginning to grow impatient and more and more frustrated with the journey. They had all been told that the trip would take two days at most, and nearly four days had already passed.

At about 3:00 p.m. that afternoon, they watched in dismay as yet another boat approached theirs. *Not again!* Doaa thought. This ship was even smaller than the one they were crammed on. The boat hardly looked seaworthy, with paint that was chipped all over and all the metal parts covered in rust. The crew of about ten men pulled up alongside their boat demanding, "Everybody switch over or we'll send you back to Egypt." The refugees, bonded by days in proximity and their common goal of reaching Italy alive, collectively refused to disembark. The new boat was just too run-down. "We've already moved so many times," one refugee complained. A parent stood up and protested, "There's no way we're getting on that boat. The children have already suffered too much!" Doaa thought of Walid's missing fingers and shuddered at the thought of switching boats again. Everyone adamantly refused to move. Confronted by the passengers' resolve, the smugglers had no choice but to oblige. A deal was struck—the passengers could remain on this boat as long as everybody agreed to stick to the story that the captain and the crew were refugees escaping the war in Syria as well and that no smugglers were on board, that they were steering the ship on their own.

The passengers readily agreed and the crew seemed relieved. The captain started up the boat again, leaving the other boat in its wake. "How much longer?" someone asked him. "Just nineteen hours and we will reach Italy," the captain assured them. The passengers cheered and clapped when they heard this. "Inshallah"—God willing—"we will make it to Italy!" they called out. Um Khalil hugged Doaa first, then Bassem. For the first time since wading into the sea, Doaa thought that they might actually make it to Europe.

NINE

All That Is Left Is the Sea

Doaa and Bassem returned to their place on the starboard side of the deck, wedging themselves between the others and settling in for the last leg of the journey. Feeling so close to their destination, people began to relax and the mood brightened a little bit. Relieved parents helped their children remove their life vests so they could be more comfortable and set them on the hard deck. The boat seemed to move faster than before over the calm sea, as passengers laughed and joked together. The sun shone bright overhead and, feeling the heat of the day, some people took refuge under plastic rice sacks that were tied together and rigged to provide shade. But Doaa remained in the sun, relishing the feeling of warmth on her face. *Nineteen more hours,* she told herself, *and all of this will be over. Then Bassem and I will be in Europe, on our way to a new life together.* The time they'd spent in jail, the miserable hours in the backs of trucks and on crowded buses, the exhausting runs through the desert, would all be worth it. She squeezed Bassem's hand and leaned her head on his shoulder. He gave her a confident smile and whispered, "We're going to make it, Doaa."

Doaa smiled at hearing this and allowed herself to close her eyes and drift asleep with the boat rocking her and the sun beating down on them. She'd only been napping a few minutes when the sounds of an engine and men shouting insults in an Egyptian dialect startled her out of sleep. By then a half hour had passed since their encounter with the other boat. She and Bassem stood up to locate the source of the conflict, grasping the side of the boat and leaning over the railing to see a blue fishing boat with the number 109 painted on its side approaching at full speed. A double-decker, it was a bigger and newer model than the boat that they were on. Doaa could see about ten men on board, dressed in ordinary clothes, not the all-black outfits of the smugglers. Some wore baseball caps to obscure their identities, but others didn't seem to care if the passengers saw their faces. Doaa had never seen pirates before, but the malevolence she saw in the men's faces brought the word to her mind.

"You dogs!" they shouted. "Sons of bitches! Stop the boat! Where do you think you are going? You should've stayed to die in your own country."

When the boat was only meters away, one of the smugglers on Doaa's boat shouted at the men, "What the hell are you doing!?"

"Sending these filthy dogs to the bottom of the sea," one of them yelled in reply. Suddenly they began hurling planks of wood at the passengers on the refugee boat, their eyes wild with hatred. The boat sped up and veered away for a moment, but then turned back toward Doaa's ship. She stared in horror as the boat sped toward them on a collision course at the spot where she and Bassem stood, clutching the side of the boat. Doaa froze with fear.

"Doaa, Doaa, put on your life vest!" Bassem's frantic voice screamed, shaking her from her paralysis. "They are going to kill us!" All around them, passengers panicked, scrambling for life jackets, as desperate prayers were interrupted by terrified shouts and children crying. The boat approaching them accelerated. Doaa had just reached for her vest when the boat rammed into the side of the ship with a shriek of metal and shattering wood just below where she and Bassem were standing. The impact was so sharp and sudden that it felt like a missile strike. Doaa stumbled forward, almost falling over the railing, but Bassem's arms shot out and grabbed her. As she was pulled back to safety, she saw that other people weren't so lucky and did fall over, landing on the hard deck and other passengers below. A scream sounded in Doaa's ear, but she couldn't tell where it had come from. Her own throat was too tight to let out a single sound. In the commotion, Doaa had dropped her life vest and couldn't find it. She scrambled around looking for it, then Bassem pulled her toward him. She realized that the boat was beginning to turn on its side. *Oh, God,* Doaa thought. *Not the water. Not drowning. Let me die now and not go into the sea.* She had one hand on the railing to keep her balance, and the other clutched Bassem's hand.

"Listen to me, Doaa," Bassem said. "Keep hold of my hand. Don't let go and we will make it. I promise I won't let you drown."

Doaa could hear the men on the attacking boat laughing as they hurled more pieces of wood at Doaa's boat. Those laughs were some of the most horrifying sounds she had ever heard. She couldn't believe they were enjoying themselves during their cruelty of trying to sink a boat carrying little children. All around her were screams of terror and people shouting desperate prayers.

The attacking boat finally reversed and pulled away from the ship, and for a moment Doaa hoped that the onslaught was over, that the men had merely wanted to frighten them. But seconds later, they sped toward them again, and Doaa understood that they had no mercy and had every intention of killing every man, woman, and child on board. This time, when they rammed the side of Doaa's boat, the rickety vessel took a sudden, violent nosedive into the sea.

Bassem's hand was yanked away from hers as he fought to regain his balance. Doaa lost sight of him in the mass of people tumbling forward. She was pressed up against the side of the boat, kept upright by the mass of people pushed up against her.

As people began to fall into the water, the men on the attacking boat jeered, calling out that each and every one of them should drown. "Let the fish eat your flesh!" they yelled as they sped away. The cold-blooded taunt echoed in Doaa's ears.

Half of the refugees' boat was already underwater and sinking fast. Doaa thought of the hundreds of people trapped in the hull. *They're doomed,* she thought as she held on to the edge of the sinking vessel, *and so are we.*

She held as tightly as she could to the side of the boat, but as it plunged downward, her fingers slipped open and she slid into the sea, immediately sinking below the surface. Doaa found herself under the plastic rice sacks that the passengers had tied together for shade on the boat. She frantically moved her arms, attempting to reach the surface, only to see that she was trapped along with dozens of other people underneath the sacks. Fighting off panic, Doaa shut her eyes, then opened them again to see the people near her struggling to free themselves from under the heavy plastic. There was no air to breathe and no path to the surface. She remembered the time her cousin had thrown her into the lake and she had breathed in heavy, choking water. This time there was no family to pull her out, nothing but cold salt water and the pressure growing in her chest and behind her eyes as she struggled to catch her breath and choked down more water. Then she saw a glimmer of sunlight and noticed a tear in the plastic. She stretched her hands into the opening, feeling as if they were moving in slow motion, and pulled herself through the small hole and above water. She gasped for air at the surface. Doaa realized that the rice sacks were still attached to the boat, and if she crawled over them, she could reach the stern—the only part that was still floating—and grab on to the edge of the boat. She made her way along the sacks, and when she reached the boat's edge, she grabbed it so tightly that she couldn't feel her hands. She caught her breath in huge gulps, then turned to look below her. The people under the plastic had stopped moving.

She heard screaming all around her, muffled only by the sound of the boat's motor. She turned her head toward the sea and saw scattered groups of people, calling out the names of their loved ones and crying for God's help. People desperately grabbed on to anything that floated—luggage, water canisters, even other people, pulling them down with them. Doaa noticed that the sea around her was colored red and realized that people were being sucked into the boat's propeller and dismembered by its blades. Body parts floated all around her. It was worse than anything she'd ever seen during the war in Daraa. She watched in horror as one moment a child was crying and struggling to hold on to the boat, then the next he lost his grip and slipped into the blades, his small body cut to pieces. There was nothing but blood and screams. She forced herself to turn away and instead shift her focus over the deck. She saw a lifeless man trapped in the metal scaffold used for fishing nets, a rope wrapped around his neck, his arms and legs cut off, his face covered in blood.

Overwhelmed with panic and fear, Doaa began shouting out desperately, "Bassem!" She was terrified that he was also one of the dead. She shouted his name over and over, all the while staring at the mangled body of the man caught in the rope. A few long seconds later, she heard Bassem's voice: "Doaa!

Doaa, don't look at him, look at me!" Doaa turned her head toward the sound of his voice and spotted him in the sea. The metal rim of the boat was cutting into her hands, and her legs dangled in the water. She wanted to go to Bassem but couldn't bring herself to jump into the water. But the boat was sinking at an angle that was drawing her toward the spinning propeller. More people were being drawn into its blades. Somehow she still could not bring herself to release her hold and allow the sea to swallow her. "Let go, or it will cut you up, too!" Bassem cried out. He tried to swim to her, but the waves bore him away.

She heard a voice beside her: "Do what he says, Doaa!" It was Walid. He was holding on to the sinking stern with his one good hand, staring at the propeller. He tore his gaze away from it and turned to Doaa, a frightened look on his face, and said, "I can't swim. I don't have a life jacket."

"I can't swim either." Her life jacket was long gone and they were both inching closer to the propeller.

Bassem cried out again: "Doaa! Jump! Now!"

"We have to let go," Doaa yelled to Walid, although she was petrified of the idea.

A look of sadness replaced the terror on his face. "Leave your hope in God," he said to her with a kindness that made her want to cry. "If you believe in God, he will save you."

She closed her eyes and opened her hands, falling backward, arms and legs spread as she hit the water's surface. She was buoyant for a few seconds on her back, then felt someone pulling at her head scarf, which slipped off her head and into the sea. As she lay floating on her back, she felt the ends of her long hair being yanked under the water. Those who were drowning below were beyond reason and grabbed at whatever they could reach for to try to pull themselves to the surface. Their hands grasped at her head, pulling Doaa's face below the water. Somehow, she managed to push their hands away. She gulped for air, turned upright, and moved her arms and legs to try to stay above water. She remembered that that was what swimming was, so she did her best to tread water as she watched the last bit of the boat sink into the waves. Nothing was left but wreckage, blood, corpses, and a few other survivors. She felt things moving beneath her and knew that they were people drowning, and that any moment one of them might grab her legs, pulling her under.

Then she spotted Bassem swimming toward her holding a blue floating ring, the kind toddlers use in baby pools and shallow seas. "Put this over your head so you can float," he said as he passed the partially inflated ring over her shoulders. Scared that someone might try to grab her legs, she pulled herself on top of the ring, her legs and arms dangling over the sides, then suddenly fainted from shock and exhaustion. Bassem splashed seawater on her face to bring her back.

The sun was starting to set over the horizon, and the sea had become still and flat, putting the scene before her in eerie focus. Survivors were gathered in small clusters, some wearing life jackets that were only keeping their heads just above water. Many of them had also been sold fake vests that could barely float. She wondered if the smugglers who gave them those life vests had intended to let them drown all along.

Bassem treaded water beside Doaa, holding on to her plastic ring. He spotted a man he recognized with a small bottle of water and begged him to give Doaa a sip. She swallowed a tiny amount, then immediately threw up all the seawater she had ingested. Getting all the salt water out of her system helped her feel more alert. She suddenly noticed all the people wailing all around them. Nearby, they heard the anguished cries of Shoukri Al-Assoulli, the Palestinian man they had met on the boat. He was floating on a plastic bag full of empty water bottles and calling out over and over the names of his wife and children: "Hiyam! Ritaj! Yaman!" With one free hand, he pushed water to the side to move up to other survivors asking, "Did you see them? My wife, my kids?" He stopped when he found another friend of his sobbing. He had also lost his wife and children. "How will I tell my mother they are gone?" he asked Shoukri.

One woman pulled out a waterproof mobile phone and tried to call any emergency number that she and others around her could think of. But there was no network. Another woman pulled her phone out of the layers of plastic bags she'd wrapped it in, finding it still dry and hoping she would have better luck. But her battery was dead.

Darkness slowly descended on the survivors floating in the water, and the sea turned black and choppy. Doaa shivered as her cold, wet clothes clung to her. The waves separated the clusters of survivors who had been holding hands, thinking that they would have a better chance of being spotted and rescued if they stuck together. Bassem clung to Doaa's water ring, and Doaa gripped his arm, terrified that he, too, would float away. Hours passed and the loud sobs of the children became weak whimpers. Doaa felt for the Quran that Walid had given her, comforted that it was still secured just above her heart. She began to recite verses out loud, and soon others around her chimed in. She felt comforted for a brief moment in this circle, and closer to God. The moon and the stars were their only light, illuminating the living and the dead. Bodies floated all around them. "Forgive me, Doaa, you shouldn't be seeing such things," Bassem apologized. But she just shook her head and held more firmly to his arm.

Approximately one hundred people had initially survived the shipwreck, but as the night wore on, more people would die from cold, exhaustion, and despair. Some who had lost their families gave up, taking off their life jackets and allowing themselves to sink into the sea. At one point Doaa heard desperate shouts as fellow passengers attempted to give hope to one young man who had removed his life jacket. "Don't do it," the other survivors pleaded. "Please don't give up." But the young man pushed the life jacket away and sank head down into the sea. He was so close to Doaa she could almost touch him.

Amid the despair, a solidarity emerged among those who were left. People with life jackets moved toward those without them, offering a shoulder to hold on to for a rest. Those with a little food or water shared it. Those whose spirits remained strong comforted and encouraged people who wanted to give up.

Bassem took off his jeans so they wouldn't weigh him down, but he was losing strength. They had been in the sea for twelve hours. "I'm sorry, Doaa. I'm so sorry," he kept apologizing. He was devastated that he had insisted they travel by sea when it terrified her so much. "It's my fault this happened. I shouldn't have made you get on the boat."

"We made this choice together," she told him firmly. His teeth were chattering and his lips had turned blue. Tears slipped down her cheeks as she saw how weak he was, but she kept her voice steady. "We're going to make it Bassem," she said, echoing the words he had used to comfort her in the boat. "We'll be rescued and we're going to have a family together."

"I swear to God, Doaa, I love you more than anyone in the world," Bassem said, clutching her hand. He crossed his arms over the edge of the float, rested his head upon them, and drifted in and out of sleep. Doaa held on to his hand as if it were the only thing keeping her from joining those the sea had taken.

When the sun rose the next day, Doaa saw that the night had taken at least half of the survivors. Corpses were floating all around her, facedown, blue and bloated. Doaa recognized some of them, but not from the group of initial survivors. She realized that they were the people who had drowned when the boat first sank, and their bodies must now have risen to the surface. The people had drowned before her eyes and throughout the night had disappeared their lungs having taken in too much water instead of air, causing their bodies to become heavy and sink. Many of the bodies that now floated in the water had their hands clutched to their chests as if they were cold. Some of the remaining survivors who had made it through the night without life jackets desperately resorted to hanging on to the corpses to keep afloat.

Doaa choked on the stench from the dead. When Bassem awoke and observed the scene around them, he began apologizing again. But this time, Doaa could hear resignation in his voice as if he had given up hope that they would survive. It sounded to Doaa as if his apologies were actually Bassem saying good-bye.

"Don't worry," Doaa assured Bassem, feeling her love for him well up in her chest. She, too, had come to accept that they might not make it much longer. "This is our fate."

A man nearby must have noticed Doaa and Bassem's spirits flagging. He yelled over to Bassem, "Keep moving or your body will go stiff!" So Bassem let go of the ring and swam off for a few minutes, looking around for something to bring Doaa—a bottle of water to moisten their parched mouths, or a box of juice to combat the dizziness that overwhelmed them both. But there was nothing but endless sea, bobbing heads, and bits of wood. He returned to Doaa, shaking his head. The sun was getting hot, which warmed their bodies but made them thirstier. Bassem was sick from all the salt water he had swallowed, so Doaa stuck her fingers down his throat to help him throw it up. Afterward, Bassem once again crossed his arms over the side of Doaa's inflatable ring and laid his head on them to rest.

A small group of survivors gathered around the couple, treading water. Some, probably delirious, were saying things that made no sense. One man said, "There is a café nearby, go get us tea!" Amid the cacophony, Bassem looked directly at Doaa, raised his voice loud enough so that everyone could hear, and solemnly declared, "I love you more than anyone I have ever known. I'm sorry I let you down. I only wanted what was best for you." Doaa saw that his eyes were feverish, and he stared into her eyes as if it was the last time he would ever see them. He spoke with an urgency she hadn't heard since he'd threatened to go back to Syria if she wouldn't agree to marry him. It was as if getting the words out was the most important thing he'd ever done. "It was my job to take care of you," he said, "and I failed. I wanted us to have a new life together. I wanted the best for you. Forgive me before I die, my love."

"There's nothing to forgive," Doaa told him, through sobs. "We will be together always, in life and in death." She pleaded with him to hold on, telling him over and over that he was not to blame.

As she reached over to stroke his cheek, she noticed an older man swimming toward them, clutching a small baby on his shoulder. He held on to a water canister with his other hand, kicking his legs hard to get closer to them. When he reached them, he looked at Doaa with pleading eyes and said, "I'm exhausted. Could you please hold on to Malak for a while?"

The baby was wearing pink pajamas, had two small teeth, and was crying. Doaa thought the baby looked just like what the name Malak meant—"angel." The man explained that he was her grandfather. He was a fisherman from Gaza, and they had left to escape the latest Israeli bombardment. Twenty-seven members of their family had been on the boat, and all the others had drowned. "We are the only two who survived. Please keep this girl with you," he begged. "She is only nine months old. Look after her. Consider her part of you. My life is over."

Doaa reached for Malak and settled her on her chest, resting the baby's cheek on the Quran that still lay next to Doaa's heart. At her touch Malak relaxed and stopped crying, and Doaa immediately took comfort in having the child's body next to hers.

Malak's grandfather touched Malak's face. "My little angel, what did you do to deserve this? Poor thing. Good-bye, little one, forgive me, I am going to die." He then swam off. Doaa and Bassem focused their attention on the small child. The young life seemed to rally Bassem for a little while as he stroked Malak's soft, cold cheeks. Moments later, Malak's grandfather returned, checking on her, and, seeing she was in good care, said good-bye again. The next time they looked in his direction, they saw him floating facedown in the sea just ten meters away.

Malak was shivering. Her lips were blue and cracked. Doaa dipped her finger in the sea and gently wet them. She thought that her own spit would be better to use, so the child wouldn't lick the salt, but Doaa had no moisture to gather from her mouth. She had heard somewhere that rubbing a person's veins along the wrists keeps the person warm, so she tried that and began to sing songs that her mother had sung to her as a baby.

Bassem also was getting lulled to sleep by Doaa's singing, and she knew that she had to keep him awake or he might just slip away from her. Doaa clapped her hands at the sides of his head to rouse him.

"I'm scared, Bassem," she told him, leaning close to his ear, "please don't leave me alone here in the middle of the sea! Hang on just a little longer and we will be in Europe together."

Doaa noticed his face was turning from yellow to blue.

He started to speak: "Allah, give Doaa my spirit so that she may live."

"Don't say that, Bassem," Doaa pleaded. "We will be together with God." But she knew he was completely exhausted and was slipping away from her. Doaa began to cry, thinking that she wouldn't be able to save him. She knew the only power left in her was her knowledge of the word of God.

"Bassem, before you die, you must swear by the Quran to be sure you die a Muslim, and that your faith goes with you," she said urgently. "Repeat after me: 'I swear that there is only one God and Muhammad is his prophet.'"

" 'I swear that there is only one God and Muhammad is his prophet,' " Bassem repeated, then closed his eyes. Doaa slapped his face to keep him awake, but he started to mutter deliriously, "Mom, the silver is for you."

He was hallucinating. To keep him engaged, Doaa decided to play along. "Okay, Bassem, when you are better, we will go and get the silver. You just stay with me and hang on. Don't leave me alone."

Doaa realized Bassem was losing consciousness, and that he had been trying to say good-bye to her. She understood that she had to give him one last gift, and through her tears, she managed to utter a promise: "I chose the same road you chose. I forgive you in this life, and in the hereafter we will be together as well." Doaa gripped Bassem's fingers with her right hand while her left arm braced Malak.

After some time, she felt his hands slip from her grasp and she watched him go limp and slide into the water. He began floating away from her, so Doaa desperately tried extending her arm to pull him back toward her, but he was beyond her reach. She couldn't get out of the inflatable ring without losing hold of Malak. "Bassem," she cried, "for God's sake, don't go! Answer me! I can't live without you." She cried out for him over and over, sobbing.

A man swam over and checked Bassem's pulse. "I'm sorry, but he's dead," he told her apathetically.

Doaa understood that, to this man, Bassem's death was just one of many; at least two dozen people had died since the sun had come up that day. But to Doaa, it was the end of everything. She had lost the most precious person in her life and she wanted to die with him. She imagined letting herself slip through the inflatable ring and into the sea with Bassem. But then she felt Malak's tiny arms around her neck and realized that she alone was responsible for this child. Doaa knew that she had to try to keep her alive.

Bassem floated facedown in the sea, then slowly began to sink beneath it. The last Doaa saw of him was his thick black hair rising up as the dark water engulfed his head. Then he was gone. She screamed just once as she witnessed this, allowing herself a moment of anguish. A man near Doaa tried comforting her. She recognized him from the boat. The man told Doaa about himself as the sun began to set on another day. He was from Damascus, he said, treading water next to her, and all he wanted was to give his son an education and a future without bombs. He started crying as he told her how he had watched, powerless, as his small son got sucked into the boat's propeller, which cut off his head. His wife had also drowned before him. "You saw it too—you saw my wife and my son die!" he screamed. *Was it his child I witnessed being cut up in the blades?* Doaa wondered.

"Don't cry," Doaa told the man, "you will be joined together in heaven."

"You are blessed," the man replied, "you don't deserve this."

Soon, more people began to move toward Doaa for comfort and prayers, but also to ask her to help them vomit up the salt water they had swallowed. Word had gone around that swallowing seawater would quicken death. They must have seen her as she helped Bassem throw up earlier that morning, and one by one, they came over to her and she used her free hand to help them vomit, washing her fingers in the sea after each turn. Though they spit up only water, the smell turned her own stomach, but their visible relief and their words of gratitude comforted her.

It was now Thursday afternoon. *I have been in this hell for two full days,* Doaa thought. She noted that only about twenty-five now survived. Malak was sleeping most of the time, but whenever she woke, she would cry. Doaa knew that even though Malak couldn't talk, she was desperate for water.

Among the other survivors was the family she had met on the boat with the two small girls, Sandra and Masa. They were all wearing life jackets, which were keeping them above water, but the older girl, Sandra, started having convulsions, her body shaking all over. Her father was holding her, speaking in a low voice through his sobs. Doaa thought she saw the girl's soul leaving her small body as she went limp. Sandra's mother, a determined look on her face, swam toward Doaa, holding the smaller girl, Masa, in both hands.

Sandra's mother grabbed on to the side of Doaa's float and looked directly into her eyes. "Please save our baby. I won't survive." Without hesitation, Doaa reached for Masa and placed her on her left side, just below Malak, who now had her head nestled under Doaa's chin. She rested Masa's head on her rib cage below her breast, and as she did so, the tiny body stretched out on her stomach. *She's not even two years old and has seen this hell,* Doaa thought, stroking Masa's hair and wondering if her small ring would keep all three of them afloat. Masa's torso was submerged in the water and the waves pushed and splashed at them.

A loud wail pulled Doaa away from her thoughts. Sandra was dead and her parents were weeping beside her floating body. Doaa held her arm tightly around Masa and tried to comfort the grieving woman with some soothing words. But just minutes later, her husband's body went slack as well. He had given up. His wife looked on in disbelief. "Imad!" she cried. Then, suddenly, she, too, went silent and passed away right before Doaa's eyes.

As night fell, the sea turned black and shrouded with heavy fog. The girls began to shift restlessly and cry, and Doaa did her best to calm them. She was afraid to move her aching arms in case she lost her grip on them. Their weight on her chest almost stopped her breathing and suppressed her constant urge to cough. She longed for water. Earlier that morning, someone had given them a bit of rich tahini halva candy found floating in the water. "The babies should have it," the stranger had said, handing it over. Doaa had broken off tiny chunks and pushed them into their open mouths. The sweet taste seemed to calm the girls. She'd saved a bit for herself, but it had only made her thirstier.

Water became an obsession for the survivors. Men urinated in empty plastic bottles and drank the liquid to stay alive. Doaa averted her eyes.

A few meters away, Shoukri Al-Assoulli was treading water near another group of survivors. Like Doaa, he had made it through the last two days, and like Doaa, he had lost everything. Now, he thought he might be losing his mind. The people around him were clearly hallucinating. One said, "Get into my car. Open the door and get into my car!" Another asked for a chair to sit down in. One man invited all the others to his house, which he said was close by.

A man named Foad Eldarma asked Shoukri to call his wife

to come and pick him up. Then he asked him to take him home to her. Another man Shoukri recognized, who was also from Gaza, swam over to Shoukri, beckoning him to come with him because, he stated with conviction, he knew a place where they could get water. Shoukri followed him a short distance, kicking his legs, but nothing was there. Another man said that he knew of a café that had all the water they wanted to drink and that they could also smoke *shisha* pipes. He said he had $100 and would pay for them all and asked, "Do you want to go?"

"Yes," Shoukri replied.

"But it will take us two hours to swim there!"

"No problem, let's go!"

A few other men joined them as they moved through the water. "We must go straight, and then at some point we have to turn left," the man instructed them. Shoukri's head cleared for a moment and he realized the man was hallucinating and so was he. He swam back to the others to join the cluster of survivors not far from Doaa's group. A cold fog wrapped around them, blinding them and making them shiver. A woman who'd lost her two daughters was sobbing. "I'm so cold. Please warm me." Shoukri and his friend Mohammad formed a circle around her to give her protection.

That night, while Shoukri dreamed that he was home with his family, he let go of the bag of water bottles that was keeping him afloat. As soon as he started to sink, he regained consciousness and grabbed on to it again. Later, he pictured himself reaching land and throwing life rings to save people, then offering them water. As the hours passed, he slipped in and out of lucidity. He wasn't sure if he was alive or dead.

Doaa wished that she could shut out the sound of the shifting sea. It was like the music in horror movies, making the scenes of death before her even more terrifying, as if the drowning of the people were set to the rhythm of the waves. Each time someone died, her heart broke. How many men had she seen take their life vests off when they decided to die? She'd lost count. *I don't blame them,* she thought, even if her religion did look down on suicide. *Their agony was too much for them to bear. And who am I to judge someone who takes his own life? I'm just a dot in this vast sea that will soon devour me, too.* If not for the strength that the two little girls on her chest gave her, she would have slipped under the waves, as well.

Doaa was exhausted but too afraid to sleep for fear that the babies might fall from her arms. She counted the corpses floating around her—seven. At least they were facedown so she didn't have to see their faces. Their shirtless backs were bloated and blue-black, the color of whales. The stench was unbearable. Each time a wave pushed a corpse into her, she pushed it away with her feet or her hand. A man named Momen helped her move some of them away. He was one of the only remaining survivors and now stuck close to Doaa.

Momen gave her strength with his words of encouragement. "You are selfless, Doaa. I've been watching how you are supporting the others. You're so brave and strong. I want to keep you safe. If we survive, I'd like to marry you."

Somehow, here, Doaa didn't find his words too forward or

strange, just caring. It was his way of keeping going, something to perhaps look forward to if they ever made it out of the water alive. Doaa replied, "Hang in there and we will talk about it later when all this is behind us."

On the morning of the third day, as the sun rose, a man, a woman, and a small boy came into Doaa's sight. The adults were holding on to an inflatable ring, just like Doaa's, which was around the boy's waist. But suddenly, the tube burst and the boy dropped into the water, his arms flailing. Doaa saw that the woman couldn't swim well. As soon as she no longer had the ring to cling to, she, too, sank below the surface, then came up for a last desperate gasp of air before her head fell forward and she was still.

The man was able to help the boy. He put the boy's arms around his neck and swam toward Doaa. "Please hold him for a while," he begged her when he reached Doaa. He was so exhausted his words were slurred. He said the boy was his nephew and that the woman who had just died was the child's mother. Doaa hesitated: "There's not enough room!" The boy was about three, bigger than the girls, and Masa and Malak would drown if the water ring sank. But the boy was looking at her in anguish and Doaa's heart went out to him. "We'll find a way," she said as she reached for him and laid him on her outstretched legs. He was wiggling and raising his head, looking around him and pleading, "I want water. I want my uncle. I want my mommy," over and over.

Doaa didn't know what to do to comfort the desperate boy and she was afraid his fussing would cause their ring to burst and they would all drown, too. Doaa wanted nothing more than to keep them all safe. The boy reminded her of Hamudi, and Doaa thought of how devastated she would be to see him drown. Again and again, the boy asked for his mother. "Your mother went to get you water and food," Doaa told him, and for a few minutes that would quiet him, but then he would complain of thirst. To soothe him, Doaa finally scooped her hand in the sea and give him salt water to drink. Over the next two hours, his uncle would swim off a short distance to keep his body moving, then swim back to check on him. He had nothing to keep him afloat. The boy began to shake and his lips turned blue; his small chest heaved up and down. His uncle, holding on to Doaa's inflatable ring, took the boy into his arms and began to cry. "Don't leave us," he begged.

The boy said weakly, "Please, Uncle, you can't die, too!" Then his body suddenly went limp over his uncle's shoulder. The man hugged the boy to his chest, pushing away from Doaa's float, and she watched as he and the little boy sank together before her eyes, while the body of the boy's mother floated next to her.

"Dear God," she heard Momen say, "everyone is dying around us. I saw my son die, and my wife. Why is this happening to us? Why did they sink us? No one is coming to save us!"

"They'll come for us, *inshallah,* Momen," Doaa told him softly. "Be strong, pray, so hope is still inside you."

But as she uttered these words, Doaa began to sob. She'd only held the little boy for a few hours, but she felt as if he'd become part of her. "They say the pain a mother feels when she loses her son is the worst in the world. I feel like that. I loved that little boy." She had seen so much death, but this last one made her feel as if her heart would crack into pieces. "It's my fault he died," she cried to Momen. "I should have been able to save him."

"No, no!" Momen replied, "It was God's will. You are good, you tried to save him."

But Doaa couldn't help feeling that she had failed the little boy. With renewed determination, she thought about how she wouldn't fail Malak and Masa. Now, nothing mattered more to her than keeping them alive.

When the girls started to stir and become agitated, she would sing to them her favorite nursery rhyme: "Come on sleep, sleep, let's sleep together, I will bring you the wings of a dove." She also invented games with her fingers to distract them. She discovered that Malak was ticklish under her chin and would laugh when she played a game in which she would use her fingers to pretend a mouse was running up Malak's chest and onto her neck. When the girls fell asleep, Doaa would rub their bodies to keep them warm, and when she thought that they might be losing consciousness, she would snap her fingers near their eyes and speak firmly, "Malak, Masa, wake up, sweethearts, wake up!"

The only word Masa said back to her was "Mama."

Doaa felt such a deep connection to these children that she began to feel as if she were their mother now. Their survival meant more to her than her own life.

In the moments when Doaa wasn't comforting the girls, she would recite the Quran, and many of the remaining survivors would gather around her to listen and pray. Some of them also knew the words of the Ayat Al Kursi, a prayer she used to recite before bed and knew by heart.

Their voices soothed the babies, and their words comforted Momen and the other survivors around her. Reciting the verses gave Doaa a sense of strength that she felt came directly from God. She clung to hope that someone would come to rescue them all soon.

On Friday, their fourth morning in the ocean, Doaa noticed that Malak and Masa were sleeping almost all the time and were barely moving. She constantly checked their pulses to make sure they were alive.

Momen became a kind of bodyguard for Doaa and the girls; protecting them gave him a sense of purpose. No other women were left among the living. The other men seeking comfort from Doaa formed a circle around them, some trying to lean on her ring for a rest. Momen would try to shoo them away, warning them, "She's carrying these kids! She could lose her balance." But Doaa would let them stay: "Lean gently, please, for the sake of the children." Momen didn't have a life jacket, but he was a good swimmer. Still, Doaa saw by late afternoon that he was beginning to lose strength.

"Don't you leave me, too!" Doaa cried, thinking he was the only adult she had left that she felt close to and trusted since Bassem had died. She didn't know what she would do without his help and comfort. Momen was floating on his back with his eyes closed when suddenly his body went still, then flipped forward, his face submerging in the sea. Doaa now felt she was completely alone except for the two children whose lives depended on her.

She was going in and out of consciousness as she lay in the ring with Malak and Masa resting on her chest. When she opened her eyes, everything looked blurry. She splashed her face with water to keep herself awake and checked to make sure that the girls were still breathing. She laid her head back again and looked up at the sky, seeing nothing but foggy shapes; then all of a sudden she thought she spotted a gleaming white plane above her head. *I must be hallucinating,* she thought, dismissing the idea. Then she thought of Bassem's words: "I pray that God would take my soul and put it in Doaa's so that she will live." She began searching the water for the spot where Bassem had died, but it all looked the same: just still water and floating corpses surrounded her. She tried to banish the thought of her beloved's body sinking below the water and getting eaten by sharks with no proper burial.

In anguish, she looked up at the sky again for any sign of a plane, but instead she only saw a small gray-and-black bird. It flew toward her and circled over her head, then glided away. The bird came back three times, and each time it seemed to look straight at her. *Could this mean land is near?* she wondered. She hadn't seen a single bird in four days, not even a seagull. *This bird must be a sign from God,* she thought. *Maybe someone will save us.*

Not long after the bird departed, she heard the sound of an engine and spotted the same white plane overhead. This time she knew she couldn't be imagining it. "Dear God!" she shouted. "Did anyone see that?" The few remaining survivors had drifted away and she was floating alone with only Malak and Masa. Two men swam toward her—Mohammad, a Palestinian she recognized, and an African man she hadn't seen before. Mohammad had a life jacket, and the African man was clutching a large plastic water canister. Doaa watched the sky and saw what looked like diamonds falling down like fireworks. Again the plane was circling above her.

"There really is a plane!" Doaa exclaimed, hopeful. "Come closer, so they see us!" she told the men.

"I don't see anything," Mohammad replied, squinting up at the sky.

"Give me your plastic bottle," Doaa commanded. When he handed it over, she held it up and angled it so that it reflected against the sun and the plane could see them. The plane started flying lower, and as it did, all three of them waved their arms, shouting, "Help! Save us!"

But then the plane suddenly disappeared and the sun fell slowly into the horizon. Doaa prayed, *Please, God, they must have seen us,* panicked at the idea of spending another night in the pitch-black water.

The sun was in her eyes now and its rays were blinding her vision, but she still kept scanning the horizon in hope. When she spotted a massive ship off in the distance, she pleaded to Mohammad, who was close by, "Stay with me, please, help me reach the ship." Doaa knew that she couldn't swim while holding the two babies.

"I can't tread water any longer," Mohammad told her, "I'm too tired. I'll swim to the ship and tell them to come here and get you."

The two men set off and Doaa watched them struggle to swim toward the boat until she could no longer see Mohammad. But the African man was still visible, and she wondered why he'd stopped all of a sudden when he was so close to being rescued, until she realized that he wasn't moving at all. He'd died just when he was about to be saved.

Night fell and Doaa could no longer see the ship or anything else in the darkness. The sea was choppy, and something crashed into the side of her ring. She turned and saw it was the corpse of the African man. His face was swollen and his eyes were open wide. Doaa screamed and pushed the body away, but the force of the current kept moving it back, smashing it into her again and again. She moved the babies to the center of her torso. Clutching them with one arm, she used all her remaining strength to paddle her free hand in the direction she last saw the boat.

But she felt that she was getting nowhere. She turned around and looked behind her. Off in the distance, she saw the lights of another big ship. She scooped some water to splash over the babies' faces to keep them awake.

How will I reach that ship? she wondered. *It is so far away. Dear God, I have the will to get there, but please give me the strength.*

She began paddling toward the boat with one hand, the other wrapped around the two little girls. She didn't care what happened to her, but if Malak and Masa lived, she felt that her life would mean something. She would last long enough to know that she had saved the little girls, then she could finally stop struggling and be with Bassem again.

TEN

Rescue at the Dying Hour

The chemical tanker *CPO Japan* was sailing across the Mediterranean toward Gibraltar when a distress call came in from the Maltese coast guard: a boat carrying refugees had sunk and all available ships were requested to provide assistance. International law requires that all ships must "render assistance to any person found at sea in danger of being lost." The captain of the *Japan* heard the call and changed course. He assigned extra lookouts to take up positions all around the cargo deck. Ship crews throughout the region regularly kept watch for refugees and migrants that had risked crossing the Mediterranean, knowing how often such attempts ended in death. The crew of the *Japan* would do whatever they could to save any survivors. But when they reached the coordinates given in the distress call, all they saw were scores of bloated corpses floating in the sea.

The ship slowed to avoid hitting the bodies. They heard

from a container ship that was already at the scene that their crew had saved five people but were about to end their rescue operation since it was getting dark. Trying to search for more bodies in the dark would be futile.

Since the start of the European refugee crisis in 2014, merchant ships had been playing an indispensable role in saving lives as unprecedented numbers of refugees and migrants attempted the dangerous journey across the Mediterranean Sea. In the year of Doaa's shipwreck, commercial vessels rescued an estimated forty thousand people. However, they are ill-equipped to operate as search-and-rescue ships, and every attempted rescue costs the shipping company time and resources.

The captain of the *CPO Japan* thought that he had done his part. He had answered the distress call, and no one would blame him for turning his ship around and continuing on course. But as he looked at the dead bodies floating around him, he decided to order the crew to release their lifeboat into the sea. *If the other boat found five people alive, perhaps there might be others,* he thought. He couldn't bear to give up when all he could see in the fading light was corpses.

A silent, determined consensus prevailed among the crew as they set about launching their search. They were just merchant seamen, men from Eastern Europe and the Philippines who had come together to man the vessel. While they weren't professional rescuers, they couldn't abandon the scene without at least trying.

The wind was picking up, the water was choppy, and

visibility was poor. Three crew members boarded a closed life-boat, and other crew cranked the pulleys to slowly release it down into the sea. This high-tech model was designed to move through rough weather on high seas and remain water-tight. They passed dozens of bobbing corpses as they set off. "Don't pick up the dead," the captain told them over the radio, "just look for survivors."

The crewmen circled the area, but found only more corpses. It seemed that their search was in vain, but suddenly the captain's voice crackled over the radio. Back on the ship, a watch-man on the bow had heard what he thought was a woman's voice calling for help. Somewhere out there, someone was still alive. The men in the lifeboat headed toward the bow, hoping to locate the source of the pleas for help.

The wind grew stronger as they continued searching, mak-ing it difficult for them to pick up anything other than roaring noise. Periodically, they would stop the boat's motor so they could hear better. Every now and again they could just make out the faint echoes of a woman's voice, but it seemed to come from a different direction every time. "Keep yelling," they shouted over and over, knowing that if she didn't, they'd never be able to find her.

After four days and nights in the water with nothing to eat or drink, Doaa's strength was failing. Her arms ached and she was so dizzy that she was afraid she would pass out. She could no longer feel her lower legs, and her throat was raw from call-ing out over and over. She wanted to give up, but the weight of

Masa and Malak resting on her chest filled her with the determination to live. She kept paddling to stay afloat, and with each push of her hand through the water, she would call out, "*Ya Rabb!*"—oh, God! But her voice seemed to disappear into the wind.

She had spotted the *CPO Japan* when it first approached, and it had seemed so close, but now she couldn't see it at all. *Where could it have gone?* she wondered as doubt began to creep up on her and she became more and more certain that she and the girls would die before anyone found them.

Then, as if Allah had at last answered her prayers, Doaa heard voices calling. She could just make out a few English words: "Where are you? Keep talking so we can follow your voice and find you!" Suddenly a wave rocked her, and the voices grew muffled, as if they were drifting farther away. Then they stopped altogether.

Doaa frantically searched her mind trying to remember the English word for *help*. When it didn't come to her, she instead used any words she knew and all her remaining strength to project them forth. *Can't they see me?* she wondered as she bobbed in the water, worried that perhaps she wasn't making any sound at all, or that she was hallucinating. But she could see that a searchlight was scanning back and forth over the waves, and each time she cried out, the light would sweep closer to her. She willed the bright beam to illuminate her float as she paddled frantically toward it. Her determination to save Malak and Masa gave her strength that she didn't know she still had.

The girls were barely moving now, beginning to lose consciousness. Doaa splashed water on their faces to keep them awake and, as quickly as she could, steered her way around the corpses and toward the sound of her only hope. She couldn't let Masa and Malak die now that rescue was so close.

Doaa's mouth was so dry that the sound coming out seemed to make a crackling noise through her lips. She wasn't sure how long she could continue shouting or keeping herself and the girls afloat. But her fear that if she stopped yelling the searchers would give up and the girls would die kept her going. Masa and Malak were both limp now, lying listless on her chest. Doaa felt as if their blood circulated through her own veins and that all their hearts were beating in unison. Their lives depended on her getting to that rescue boat. *Once Masa and Malak are safe,* she thought, *I can go back to the spot where Bassem drowned and be with him again.* The thought that she only had to last a little while longer and then she could rest and be with Bassem comforted her.

Finally, after two hours, a sailor looking out of the window of the lifeboat cried, "I see her!" Suddenly, the spotlight swiveled toward Doaa. A futuristic red capsule the size of a small bus floated before her, like something out of a movie. At first she thought she was imagining it; it looked nothing like any other boat she'd ever seen. Men on the boat gazed down at her in astonishment, shocked to see such a slight young woman afloat on an ordinary inflatable beach ring, her bottom half submerged underwater.

A side door swung open and something that looked like an entry to a cage emerged from it. A man at its entrance called to Doaa and extended a pole to her. Doaa grabbed it and held on tight as they pulled her and the girls in. As she neared the boat, Doaa spoke to the men at the other end of the pole, her voice weak but her tone urgent, but she soon realized they didn't understand a word she was saying.

When Doaa finally reached the boat, the men grabbed her arms and legs to try to hoist her inside with them, but she resisted. With the last of her voice, Doaa pleaded in Arabic to her rescuers that they had to save Malak and Masa. Frantically she pointed at her chest and lifted her thin jacket to reveal the two small children lying on her chest, her weak arm clasped around them. The men were astonished. Not only had this fragile-looking young woman survived when so many others had died, but she had somehow kept two young children alive as well. One of the officers of the ship, Dmytro Zbit-nyev, pulled the first child out of Doaa's arms, then the second, and carefully handed them to his fellow crew members, who wrapped them in thermal blankets and clutched them in their arms, their tiny lives so precious amid so much death. Finally, Dmytro reached down to pull Doaa into the boat. But again she resisted.

I love these girls so deeply. Please let them be all right, she thought as she pictured Malak's sweet two-toothed smile. *At least they are safe now and I don't have to fight for them any-more. Now I can join Bassem.* On her own for the first time in days and filled with a sense of relief that she had fulfilled her duty, Doaa drew her knees up to push away from the boat. *I want to go back to Bassem and die with him.* Doaa wasn't sure if she had said it out loud or not.

At that moment, one of the crew members reached for her leg, drawing Doaa in closer so that they could pull her up into the boat and into the warm cabin. She was delirious with thirst and exhaustion and had begun to lose track of what was real and what was just her imagination. *I can't stand living without him,* she thought to herself. But even as she resigned herself to perishing in the sea with Bassem, she was too weak to resist the men who were trying to save her. Even heavy with complete exhaustion, Doaa still didn't weigh much, and Dmytro easily lifted her up into the boat and carefully laid her on the floor. Doaa was immediately wrapped in a blanket and someone placed a wet sponge to her lips so she could draw moisture from it. Tasting the freshwater, she felt thirstier than she had ever been in all those days she was afloat in the sea. She signaled for more and tried to reach her hand to the water bottle, but she couldn't move it. A man brought a straw to her cracked lips so she could fill her mouth with the clear liquid and draw it all into her parched body. The water tasted heavenly, but Doaa gulped it so quickly that she vomited.

Meanwhile, Masa and Malak were not moving. "We have to do everything we can to keep them alive!" Dmytro ordered his colleagues before radioing the chief officer on the ship to alert the coast guard and request a rescue helicopter. Dmytro looked around him in astonishment and would later ask, "Is this a miracle? Or destiny? For merchant seamen like us who aren't trained in search and rescue to find a person in such conditions at sea is like finding a needle in a haystack. And with the bad weather, there is no way they would have survived another hour on that little ring."

Doaa lay limp in the lifeboat, weak, emaciated, and unable to move a muscle as they made their way back to the *Japan*. She could feel the waves pushing the lifeboat against the big ship as it took several attempts before it could be lifted and secured back on the ship. When they finally boarded the *Japan*, the men carried her out and carefully laid her on a stretcher. She lost sight of Masa and Malak but instead saw curious, worried, and kind eyes all around her. No one spoke Arabic, but they understood when she told them she was not Masa's or Malak's mother.

Doaa lay on the stretcher shivering in her wet clothes. A man held out a crisply ironed orange coverall, just like the one that all the crew members were wearing. She somehow managed to communicate that she wanted to dress herself and in private. They seemed to understand and formed a circle around her with blankets, with their backs to Doaa, so she could discreetly peel off her wet clothes as she sat on the deck and pulled on the coverall. It took all her remaining strength to get it on her body. As she brushed her hand over her pounding head, her fingers grazed over the white scrunchie that tied her hair back. She remembered the smile on Bassem's face when he had given it to her, the thought of which made her cry. Overcome with emotion and suddenly feeling exposed, Doaa longed for a scarf to cover her hair. She had never before been in front of men outside her family with her head uncovered. Seeking comfort, Doaa felt around her neck for another gift that had meant so much when Bassem had first given it to her. The charms that dangled from her beloved necklace were of a Syrian opposition flag and a spent bullet that Bassem had collected in Daraa before he'd fled.

Pulling herself together, Doaa examined the pile of clothes and the documents she had so carefully wrapped in plastic that lay around her. These were her only remaining belongings, and she was relieved that they were still intact. One by one, with all the trust she had left, she handed them to one of the men who had pulled her from the water: Bassem's and her passports, their engagement contract, the five hundred euros in rolled-up bills, her mobile phone, and her precious Quran. Then she collapsed back onto the deck, the last of her strength gone. The crew members helped her back onto the stretcher and carried her belowdecks into a small room. Carefully, they lifted her onto a cot and laid a soft pillow under her head, then covered her with a warm blanket.

The nearest coast guard station was in Greece on the island of Rhodes, too far away for a rescue helicopter to reach the tanker's present location. The crew instead received instructions to head toward the Greek island of Crete so that the helicopter could meet them on the southwestern shore. It would take at least four hours to get to that meeting point and to the medical help that Doaa and the girls desperately needed. The captain looked out to sea, then put the engines at full speed.

Meanwhile, belowdecks, members of the crew were taking care of Masa, Malak, and Doaa with all the first-aid knowledge they had. A man peeled the wrapper off a chocolate bar and offered it to Doaa. She let it melt on her tongue. It tasted wonderful, but the sugar suddenly caught in her throat and she started to cough uncontrollably and her breath became short. Someone placed an oxygen mask over her face and she soon relaxed. She felt as if she were still bobbing in the sea, and when she opened her eyes, she could hardly believe that she was on a ship, safe and alive.

Doaa drifted in and out of sleep that night. At one point she awoke to find that the crew were taking photos and selfies with her. But she didn't mind. She knew they were good people and felt safe with them around her. God had delivered her to them, she thought, as she dozed off again. Doaa was beset with dreams of drowning and choking and at least once she woke up gagging. In her dream she was trapped underwater, trying to reach the surface for air. She awoke with a start and was surprised to find one of the men in her room setting down her clothes beside her bed. They were washed, meticulously ironed, folded, and smelled like fresh soap. The man then carefully placed her documents, money, and her Quran on top of her T-shirt and slipped everything into a plastic bag. This small gesture of kindness comforted Doaa, and she lay back on her cot and closed her eyes again.

As Doaa fought off nightmares, the crew were desperately trying to save the little girls. One crew member spoke on the radio to a doctor from the Maltese coast guard who was giving him guidance. Since there was no medic on board, the crew had resorted to their minimal first-aid training. The crew member told the doctor that both children looked bad—they remained unconscious, their breathing was shallow, and their body temperatures were dangerously low. Doaa was also in bad shape; she was weak and could only speak slowly and unintelligibly. But the little girls seemed on the brink of death. The doctor advised the crewman to offer only small sips of warm water and to wrap the babies in blankets with hot-water bottles inside. The girls were probably suffering from hypothermia, and their bodies needed to warm up slowly. A watchman was assigned to monitor their breathing and to keep taking their temperature.

Five hours after she was pulled from the water, Doaa could hear the noise of a helicopter overhead. Stirring from sleep, she found crew members rushing into her room, gesturing to her that it was time to leave. She attempted to stand, but her legs buckled under her weight and she dropped back down on the bed. Six men surrounded the cot and lifted it up with her in it, carrying Doaa to the top deck. There the helicopter hovered above, dangling a collapsible rescue basket that slowly dropped to the deck. The bottom of the basket was a square metal-and-rope frame attached to a cable by a web of thick ropes with rubber buffers. When pulled taut, the ropes formed a strong, pyramid-like cage. The wind whipped through Doaa's hair and she felt a chill as a man wearing a vest and a helmet picked her up and folded her into the basket. She was so weak, she couldn't sit up. The man knelt next to her at the opening, holding on to the ropes and smiling at her reassuringly as they rose to the hovering helicopter. Feeling safe cocooned in the basket, she looked down at the black, choppy water. She thought, *I can never hate the sea again because Bassem is a part of it now.* She recalled some of his last words: "If I die, all I want is for you to be happy."

A pair of strong arms reached down from the belly of the helicopter to pull her into the cabin. Doaa was surprised to discover that other survivors were already inside. The first one she saw was Mohammad—the man who had swum toward the first rescue boat with the African man trailing him earlier that day, promising to return for her but never coming back. That boat hadn't been an illusion after all. "You're here," he said without emotion when he saw her. Doaa averted her eyes. She had nothing to say to the person who had not come back to save her. Then she noticed Shoukri, the devastated Palestinian who'd lost his wife and two small children just after the boat had sunk. He was sitting in silence and staring through the window out to the sea. She recognized two other men but couldn't recall their names. And nestled in the arms of one of the helicopter crew was little Masa, wrapped tightly in a white fleece blanket. Her tiny bare feet were sticking out at the end, flopping to the side. She wasn't moving at all. *Please, please, let her be alive,* Doaa prayed. She frantically scanned the benches for Malak but couldn't find her. Maybe she was about to be pulled up next from the ship, Doaa thought. But then the door closed and the helicopter lurched forward. No other survivors were brought on board. Doaa caught the attention of one of the helicopter's crew. "Malak?!" she cried desperately. "The baby?!"

But it was too loud in the helicopter and she couldn't quite make out the man's response, and even if she could, he was speaking English. She asked again, and this time one of the other survivors translated for her. Little Malak had died, he relayed to Doaa. The crew did everything they could to resuscitate her, but she was gone. Doaa's breath caught in her throat as she heard this news and she began to sob. She felt as if her heart were being torn out of the exact spot on her chest where Malak had nestled her head. Doaa couldn't stand the unfairness of it. Malak had survived four days in the water only to die after being rescued. Doaa would rather she had died and Malak had lived. Racked with grief, Doaa wondered whether the baby would have survived if only Doaa had insisted on keeping her safe in her arms as Doaa sang songs and recited verses from the Quran, just as she had done in the water. A doctor approached Doaa looking concerned and feeling for her pulse. Then he turned abruptly away and quickly made his way over to Masa, laying her flat on her back and starting CPR, the heel of his hand pressing down on her chest. Doaa held her breath. She couldn't bear to lose Masa, too. After a few tense moments, the doctor stopped the chest compressions and sat back with a relieved smile. Masa was breathing again, and a faint hope flickered in Doaa's heart.

After an hour, the helicopter landed at a military base near the port city of Chania in western Crete. Two ambulances were waiting outside. As the sun began to rise on the horizon, Doaa was lifted onto a stretcher and carried away.

When she awoke, Doaa was in a hospital bed and a policeman was at her bedside speaking in a language she'd never before heard. Next to him was a man about her father's age who spoke to her in Arabic with an Egyptian accent. He asked for her name and where she was from, explaining that she was safe in a Greek hospital. He began translating the policeman's questions: Where did the boat leave from? Who was on it? How many? Where were they going? Who were the smugglers? How did it sink? The questions made Doaa dizzy and she wanted to go back to sleep. She told them as quickly as she could manage that a gang of evil men intentionally sank the boat and that almost all of the five hundred passengers had drowned. The policeman asked Doaa if the girls she was rescued with were her daughters. When she shook her head, he asked, "How come they're not yours?" She thought that was a strange question, but explained that the baby that was still alive was Masa and that she was from Syria like Doaa, and that the other girl, Malak, was from Gaza and was the only survivor of her family of twenty-seven who had also been on the boat, but that she had died. Through a stream of tears, Doaa told them that the girls had been entrusted to her by their families and she'd tried to keep them alive. Overcome again with sadness as she thought of Malak's passing, Doaa sobbed and sobbed before falling back into a long sleep.

The next time she woke up, Doaa saw that she was now in a large hospital room with other patients. She peeled off her blankets, looked down at her arms and legs, and saw that they were covered in ugly purple-and-black bruises. Doaa tried to stand to go to the toilet, but she fell over. As she attempted to pull herself up from the floor, a sharp pain ripped through her legs, and she wondered if she had lost the ability to walk. Besides the pain in her legs, the muscles in Doaa's arms ached from having held Masa and Malak for so long in the same position. A nurse hurried over to Doaa and carefully eased her into a wheelchair and pushed her to the bathroom. Doaa signaled for privacy, and the nurse closed the door. Once alone, Doaa lifted herself with both hands and leaned heavily on the sink, peering at her reflection in the mirror. She almost didn't recognize her own face. It was sunburned and peeling, and her eyes looked as if they belonged to a stranger who was staring back at her with a forlorn expression. She raked her fingers through her disheveled hair and large clumps came out in her hand. Doaa must have screamed because the nurse threw open the door and entered with a worried look. She helped Doaa back into the wheelchair and brought her back to her bed. Doaa was relieved to get away from the haunting reflection of herself in that mirror.

Back in bed, Doaa thought of calling her mother, but had no idea what she would say. How could she tell her what had happened? Besides, she felt too dizzy and disoriented and wasn't able to remember any phone numbers. Doaa reached for her mobile phone and tried to turn it on, but it was dead. She stared at it and thought, *I feel like I'm dead, too, even though I am alive.*

Little Masa had been taken to another clinic, Crete's University Hospital in Heraklion, where she was in the pediatric unit's intensive care station. Dr. Diana Fitrolaki, who oversaw Masa's treatment, said that Masa was on the verge of death when she arrived. She was suffering from acute kidney failure, hypothermia, and severe dehydration. She was lethargic and semiconscious. The doctor worried that if she did survive, she would have brain damage. The hospital had never seen a case like Masa's before, and the staff worked around the clock to do everything they could to save her. She was put on mechanical ventilation and an IV to restore her glucose and liquid levels. The staff named her Nadia and would often take her into their arms and sing songs to her, never leaving her alone.

Soon the press arrived, and Masa's fight for life became a top news story in Greece. A photo of her in her hospital bed, looking into the camera with wide, sorrowful eyes, was printed in the papers and appeared online. On the fourth day after the rescue, hospital director Nikos Haritakis spoke to the media: "The child battled the waves for days and nights. When she came here, she was completely dehydrated, burnt by the sun, and suffering a multitude of biochemical imbalances. Yet she was taken off mechanical support in just four days. Today she has excellent awareness of her environment, is eating and drinking normally, and is in very good shape. A child as young as her could have suffered irreversible brain damage from the dehydration."

As soon as the news broke that the miracle baby had survived the shipwreck as well as four days in the water, the hospital switchboard was abuzz with calls from Greek families wanting to adopt her. Director Haritakis estimates there were as many as five hundred offers. No one could resist the tiny child who had survived against such incredible odds.

Meanwhile, after four days of treatment, Doaa was slowly recovering, physically at least. She was transferred to a home for the elderly to recuperate further. The media was calling Doaa a heroine for saving baby Nadia and for surviving so long in the Mediterranean. The Egyptian man who had translated for her when she first awoke in Greece came to see her often, bringing his wife with him. They brought her clothes and offered to take her into their home. They had four daughters, one of whom was also Doaa's age. She would be welcome and no trouble, the couple assured her, and besides, she was alone in a new country and would need protection. As an alternative, the Greek authorities offered to provide her with a small apartment, a stipend, and the chance to seek asylum.

Doaa knew she was in no condition to live alone in a foreign country, so she decided to take up the Egyptian family's offer, and after two days at the elder-care home, she moved into their apartment in Chania. They had set up a bed for her in their girls' room. The modest, cozy home, the familiar rituals, and Egyptian home cooking soon soothed Doaa.

However, she knew that her parents must be worried sick.

They hadn't heard from her in more than a week, and Doaa had been too sick and disoriented when she was in the hospital to try to reach them. Every time she picked up the phone, she struggled to remember their phone numbers, and when she thought of what she would say, the idea of articulating what had happened to her and Bassem exhausted her and all she wanted to do was sleep. But she knew she had to call them eventually. Doaa racked her brain for their number or any of her sisters' or friends' numbers, but she couldn't recall a single one. Then she had the idea to remove the SIM card from her dead phone and insert it in one that her hosts had given her. She remembered that when she had sent photos to friends via the messenger service WhatsApp, the phone number of the recipient would appear above the photos. On her new phone, she opened the messenger service and scrolled to the contacts list. The first number she saw of someone who could be helpful was of one of her friends in Egypt. She dialed the number, but it was the middle of the night and no one answered. Feeling slow and tired, Doaa continued scrolling through her phone. At last, she found a photo that her sister Ayat, who was now living in Lebanon, had sent to her. Above the photo was Ayat's number, which Doaa immediately dialed.

After several rings, she heard her sister's sleepy "Hello?"

"Ayat, this is Doaa!" It was still a strain to speak and Doaa's voice sounded strange to her from all the screaming for help.

"Doaa! Where have you been?" Ayat sounded relieved, and Doaa almost starting crying at the sound of her voice. She told Doaa their mother had phoned two days ago, desperate to know if she had heard anything from her sister. That was the first time Ayat had learned that Doaa and Bassem had been on a boat to Italy that should have arrived long ago. Ayat had been worrying ever since.

"Where is Bassem?"

"Bassem is sleeping at the mosque because we are all girls here and he can't stay with us," Doaa lied. She just couldn't bring herself to tell her older sister that Bassem had died. Speaking the words would make it real. She abruptly told Ayat that she had to hang up as she was using a borrowed phone.

"You need to call Mom and tell her you're okay!"

"I'll call her, but I can't remember her number. Please give it to me and I will," Doaa promised before quickly getting off the phone.

Doaa couldn't think straight and didn't sleep the rest of the night, worrying what she would tell her family about Bassem. She couldn't even remember anymore what was real and what she had imagined. For days, all she had thought about was surviving and keeping the little girls alive. But now she didn't know what she should do next. Masa and Malak had given her a sense of purpose; now she had none. Before, all of her plans had been about building a life with Bassem. Now she was alone. If she talked to her parents, she would have to admit he was gone, and that meant she would have to figure out how to live without him and also confront her feeling that she was responsible for his death. When Bassem had wanted to turn back during their bus ride to the boat, she had insisted that they forge ahead, despite her own premonitions.

When she knew she couldn't wait any longer, she picked up the phone to call her mother.

From the moment Hanaa and Shokri said good-bye to Doaa and Bassem, they were filled with worry. Hanaa had a foreboding that she would never see them again. After Doaa's last call letting her parents know that she and Bassem were about to reach the beach from which the boat would leave, Hanaa and Shokri had stayed inside at home as much as they could, avoiding anyone who might ask whether they had any news. After five days passed with no word, Hanaa was beside herself with worry. The trip should have taken four days at most. She phoned Doaa's friends and asked them to check "Fleeing from Death to Death," a Facebook page that tracked refugee boat journeys to Europe and published announcements when a boat arrived safely. Many boats were listed on the page, but not the one that had left Gamasa on September 6.

Hanna tried telling herself that they had made it and just hadn't found a way to contact her yet. Or perhaps the boat had had engine trouble at sea and they were waiting for rescue. Shokri wondered aloud whether, as before, they hadn't made it to the boat and were unable to call from prison. The one thing neither would say to the other was that Doaa and Bassem may have died at sea.

Conflicting information began to come in through friends and family. On the way to the store, Nawara heard a rumor that the boat had sunk, but that Doaa and Bassem were among two hundred survivors. Another time, neighbors told Saja that Doaa and Bassem were dead. The sisters kept these rumors to themselves, for fear of panicking their parents.

About six days after she'd last heard from Doaa, Hanaa also got wind of a rumor that the boat had sunk and there were no survivors. She began to fear the worst, but remained silent, not wanting to worry her family or admit to herself that Doaa could be dead. Then, on September 18, twelve days after Doaa and Bassem had left, a group of neighbors knocked on Hanaa and Shokri's door, asking to come in, saying that they had some news. From the looks on their faces, Hanaa knew it was about Doaa and Bassem, but she was afraid to ask. The women moved out to the balcony and the men sat gloomily in the adjacent living room.

Just as they were about to speak, Hanaa's phone rang. She reached for it, relieved to break the tense silence and delay the news she sensed they were about to tell her. "Who's calling and what do you want?" she said, uncharacteristically abrupt.

"Mom, it is Ayat! Listen! Doaa is alive!" Ayat quickly told her mother about the 3:00 a.m. call that she had received and that Doaa was safe with a family in Greece.

"Thank God!" Hanaa was weak with relief.

Hanaa told Ayat that she had days ago heard that there had been a shipwreck but had kept the news to herself, not wanting others to worry. Then Hanaa asked about Bassem.

"She told me he was sleeping in a mosque, but she sounded odd," Ayat said. "I'm not sure. She was disoriented when we spoke, but something about what she said sounded wrong." Ayat gave Hanaa Doaa's number in Greece so she could speak to Doaa herself.

Hanaa dialed the number as soon as she got off the phone with Ayat. A woman answered, speaking Arabic. Hanaa anxiously asked to speak to her daughter.

After a few long seconds, Doaa picked up the phone. "Mom, I'm okay. I will call you when I am feeling better." She sounded faint and distant.

Hanaa was flooded with relief, but couldn't believe that Doaa was going to hang up so quickly. "Where is Bassem?"

"He's at the supermarket," Doaa said flatly.

Hanaa could sense something was wrong in Doaa's reply and hastiness to get off the phone. Hanaa asked to speak to Doaa's hostess again. When the woman came back on the line, Hanaa pressed her for details. "She's fine," the host mother said, promising that the family would treat Doaa as their own daughter and protect her. When Hanaa asked about Bassem, the woman would only say that he was away, but gave no other details. Hanaa guessed from the woman's strained tone that Doaa was nearby, so Hanaa asked if they could speak in private. A few moments passed, then the woman began to speak more frankly. She told Hanaa she suspected Bassem had drowned along with most of the other passengers and that Doaa was in denial. The woman said Doaa was a heroine who'd survived four days in the water and had saved a baby girl. "Doaa has a kind heart and she is safe with us. Be thankful to God she is alive." Then the woman whispered to Hanaa, "May Bassem rest in peace," and offered to put Doaa back on the phone.

Doaa's voice was so faint it was hard to recognize it was her.

All Hanaa wanted to do was cry, but she knew she needed to be strong for Doaa. "Say something, my daughter, so your father and our neighbors can hear it is you." By this time, family and friends had congregated around Hanaa after hearing that Doaa was alive. Hanaa put the phone on speaker and told her, "Everyone is here, asking about you."

"I'm okay," Doaa assured everyone huddled in the room, the most response she could manage.

Everyone burst out crying at the sound of her voice.

"Rest, Doaa," Hanaa told her, promising to call again the next day.

Every night, nightmares rattled Doaa awake. She kept seeing Bassem slipping away from her into the sea. As these dreams came to her over and over, she wrestled with accepting them as fact. Slowly, the reality that Bassem was dead sank in, and during the day when Doaa was mainly left home alone, she was consumed by grief.

Some days she would go out on the apartment's balcony, look up at the sky, and imagine Bassem there. "If only you were here with me today!" she'd say with her face tilted toward the

clouds, hoping in vain for a response. "My happiness is broken without you." Other days, Doaa would pretend that Bassem was still alive. In one daydream, she would imagine meeting
him walking down the main shopping street in Chania, where
they would embrace and resume their love story where they
had left off. She still couldn't bring herself to admit his death
to her family. During one of her phone calls with her parents,
Shokri asked how she was coping with Bassem's death, and
Doaa replied without thinking, "He's not dead, Papa, he's
alive."

Meanwhile, word was spreading through Arabic social media about the young woman who'd survived one of the worst
refugee boat shipwrecks in the Mediterranean and saved a baby
girl. Friends and family of missing passengers were anxiously
looking for news of their loved ones, and Doaa's story gave
them hope. A friend of her host family's published their phone
number on a Facebook page for anyone looking for information about the wreck. Within minutes, hundreds of messages
and calls started pouring in. "Do you know what happened to
my daughter?" "Is my son alive?" "Did my mother survive?"
"Here is a picture of my sister; did you see her?" "Did you see
my father?" "Did you see my uncle?" "Did you see my friend?"
The messages overwhelmed Doaa, but she did her best to reply to them, asking people to send photos so she could see if
she recognized anyone. How could she tell them all there was
no hope? That she knew of only six survivors, including herself,
here in Greece, and five others who had been taken to Malta?

But that was all. How could she tell them that she did recognize some people, but that it was from when she had watched them drown?

Some of the messages were ugly: "How come you are one of the only ones who survived? You must have been helped by the smugglers." Reading through the onslaught of messages exhausted Doaa, each one reminding her of the deaths she'd witnessed and reviving her sadness at losing Bassem and Malak. Then one text message, from a Mohammad Dasuqi, caught her eye: "Doaa, I think you saved my niece Masa." A photo was attached of a baby girl in a blue dress with white pansies. Doaa looked closely at the picture. The toddler smiling at the camera was indeed the same Masa that Doaa had cradled in her arms for four days at sea.

Doaa held out the phone to her host mother and exclaimed, "Masa has a family!" With a huge smile on her face, Doaa felt a surge of happiness for the first time since the shipwreck. She replied to the message immediately, relieved to finally be able to give someone some good news: "Yes, that is the same Masa who was rescued with me!"

Doaa learned that Mohammad Dasuqi was the twenty-eight-year-old brother of Masa's father, Imad, and was living as a refugee in Sweden with Masa's oldest sister, Sidra, who was eight. He had only had enough money for the two of them to go to Europe and had applied to bring the rest of the family, including his own wife and infant daughter and Sidra's parents and siblings, to Sweden through family-reunification procedures. But after a year had passed with no papers, Masa's father had grown tired of waiting and decided to take matters into his own hands and book passage for his family. He believed that since Mohammad and Sidra had made it safely, the rest of the family was certain to reach Europe as well. Before boarding the boat, he had taken a picture of Sandra and Masa standing side by side, wearing bright orange life vests, Sandra's arm slung confidently around Masa's shoulders. He had sent the photo to his brother confident that they would soon be together again.

When Mohammad heard of the shipwreck, and that almost everyone on board had died, his heart sank. He knew that his brother, his sister-in-law, and their little girls were on that boat and that they were most likely dead. Then he read about the nineteen-year-old Syrian woman who had survived and saved a two-year-old girl. He saw a picture of the rescued child and compared it to the photo he had. Masa was alive!

The day after Doaa texted Mohammad confirming that Masa was safe, he flew to Crete, arriving at the hospital and demanding to see his niece. It would take almost a year for UNHCR and the Swedish embassy in Athens to confirm that Mohammad was related to Masa and to recognize him as her legal guardian so as to finalize reunification. During that time, Masa was cared for in an orphanage in Athens that specialized in treating traumatized children. She played with the other children and quickly learned to speak Greek. After DNA tests and court hearings, Masa was finally able to join her uncle, aunt, older sister, and a cousin, who had since joined him, to start a new life in Sweden.

• • •

Finding Masa's family was a turning point for Doaa. The experience made her feel as if her heart might begin to heal. At fleeting moments she even believed she could be reunited with her own family and begin her life anew. But the news from home was grim. In the weeks after her rescue, media outlets from around the world had requested interviews with Doaa, questioning her about the circumstances of the shipwreck. A number of stories quoted her accusing the smugglers of ramming her boat, and of being responsible for the deaths of five hundred people. She didn't understand the reach—or consequences—that these interviews would have until she received a distressed call from her mother.

"Someone threatened me, Doaa!" Hanaa told her in the same frightened tone that Doaa had last heard from her mother when the Egyptian men had threatened to rape Doaa and her sisters. "He said, 'Tell Doaa to shut her mouth and to stop naming names. We know where you live.'"

It had been the first of many calls from unknown numbers, each one threatening to harm Doaa's family.

Hanaa told Doaa she'd reported the calls to the police and contacted UNHCR, which took the threats seriously. They sent someone to talk to the family and advised them to change apartments. "I don't want to move again," Hanaa admitted to Doaa. Doaa assured her mother she wouldn't give any more interviews, and they hoped that the men would leave them alone.

But a few days later, Doaa received another anguished call from her mother. She'd been home with the family when she'd heard a knock at the door. An elegantly dressed Egyptian man stood outside, politely asking for their passports, saying he was a police officer. Without thinking, Hanaa had retrieved the documents and handed them over. He flipped through them, reading the names aloud. "That's when I became suspicious," she told Doaa. Hanaa snatched the passports out of the man's hands, asking him, "Why did you want our passports?"

"I was just checking if there are any Syrians here," he said, then left abruptly. After he departed, Hanaa went to the local police station asking whether they had sent an officer to her place to check IDs. When they told her they hadn't, Hanaa was worried. What if she had put the family in harm's way? she wondered. Then she received a text message full of obscenities that said, "I know the names of your daughters."

Not long after that, Saja and Nawara were walking home when they sensed that they were being followed. They turned to look behind them and spotted a tall, nicely dressed man with what looked like a knife in his right hand. They recognized him as the person who had come to their door asking for their passports and posing as a policeman. Terrified, they quickly crossed the street and joined a neighbor they knew who was nearby. Later, when the girls told Hanaa and Shokri what had happened, the family realized they had no choice but to move. Hanaa called UNHCR again, and legal officers visited them to learn more. She told them the entire story of what had happened to Doaa and the threats, including the sexual harassment the girls were facing, which forced Hanaa and Shokri to pull them out of school. The UNHCR officer told the family that they were qualified for UNHCR's resettlement program due to their precarious situation. Sweden was one of the countries accepting "vulnerable" Syrian refugees. "Sweden," Hanaa said, "that's where Doaa and Bassem wanted to go."

Doaa was determined to do everything she could to get her family out of Egypt. Her anger at the people who were threatening them temporarily shook her out of her grief and into action. She turned to UNHCR's Erasmia Roumana, a caseworker Doaa had come to trust, for help. The process would be long and complex, Erasmia explained. While Doaa's family would have a strong case, Greece had no established resettlement program with another EU country. Erasmia explained that Doaa had the option of applying for asylum in Greece. If she received it, she could settle there and have the right to travel and eventually apply for citizenship. But Doaa's heart was set on Sweden; she and Bassem had planned to make a life together there. If she couldn't get there with Bassem, she'd get her family there, and if she couldn't get her family there, then she would have to go by herself. Once in Sweden, she would carry out her and Bassem's original plan alone—to apply to the Swedish family-reunification program and bring her family to join her.

Every day Doaa struggled with despondency, but fighting for her family's safety gave her a new resolve, and over the next few months her life began to come together. Her story had captured the imagination of Greek civil society. The mayor of Chania called on national authorities to grant her Greek citizenship for her heroism. Unfortunately, nothing came of it, but the request helped Doaa see herself in a new light—as someone who was brave and strong.

Then, on December 19, 2014, the prestigious Academy of Athens presented Doaa with their annual 3,000-euro award for her courage. Her visit to Athens and the pride she felt in accepting the award felt like a watershed moment, and she began to look to the future. She told herself that she would not stop fighting until she was reunited with her family. After that she would study to become a lawyer, so she could fight for justice. She had seen too little of it in her life.

In pain from being away from her family, she struggled to overcome the despair and grief that would at times engulf her spirit. For the first nineteen years of her life, she had always been surrounded by family. Now that she was on her own, she found it easier to be alone with her memories than to share them. She felt different from girls her age, and while she enjoyed the company of her host sisters who were kind to her, she knew they could never understand what she had been through. She couldn't find the words to express the horror of the deaths and suffering she had witnessed or the depth of her own grief. Her sorrow threatened to overwhelm her whenever she tried to talk about it. After the evil she had seen, it was hard to trust people again. Doaa felt that she could help herself and never turned to anyone else for aid in overcoming her trauma.

At times during the ordinary rituals of everyday life, a sudden memory from her days in the water would hit her so powerfully that the pain would come back all over again. One day, as she was brushing her hair and looking in the mirror, she smelled Bassem's cologne and swung around to see if he was standing behind her. Friends back in Egypt told her of rumors that he was alive and in a prison there. Part of her wanted to believe it was true, although almost every night her mind replayed the scene of his drowning before her eyes. She tried to think of ways she could have kept him alive. It would take her hours to return to sleep after that, and the next morning when she woke, she would hope the visions of his death had just been a dream and that he would be waiting for her outside her door.

In the summer of 2015, almost one year after she had been rescued, Doaa was still struggling with her grief, nightmares, and the fear that she would never move forward with her life. One day she watched a news story about the thousands of refugees from her country that were arriving in Greece. They had crossed the sea from Turkey and were making their way through the Balkans to Austria, Germany, and Sweden. She often thought of taking her prize money and paying another smuggler to help her travel to Sweden like the other refugees. But staff at UNHCR who were working to help resettle Doaa warned her that the journey was dangerous, especially for a young woman traveling alone. They urged her to be patient for another solution. They were working on resettling her family to Sweden, and finding a way for her to join them. When the paperwork went through, Doaa could fly to Sweden and legally restart her life alongside her family. Doaa found it almost impossible to remain patient or to trust anyone who promised to help, but if it meant that she might get her family to safety, she would try. Until then, she would heal in the cocoon of her host family.

One day that summer, after a year of struggling with grief, nightmares, and the fear that she would never move forward with her life, Doaa joined her host family on a picnic at the beach. After they finished eating, on an impulse Doaa stood up, kicked off her sandals, and walked into the shallow sea until it reached her shoulders. The water was clear and cool and still. She stood there holding her breath, then calmly let her body sink down until the water covered her head for a few moments. When she came out and returned to the shore, she turned back to look out at the horizon and thought, *I am not afraid of you anymore.*

Epilogue

Doaa was safe in Crete, and she was healing, but she soon began to grow restless, worrying about her future. The Greek government offered her the opportunity to apply for asylum. Yet despite the kindness of the people around her, Doaa didn't feel like Greece was her home. Every day that she was there she had to face the sea where Bassem had drowned, and although the sight of it no longer filled her with dread, she wanted to move away from everything it reminded her of. She and Bassem had always dreamed of making it to Sweden, and she wanted to fulfill that dream. At the same time, Doaa was also terrified for her family; the threats from the smugglers were escalating, and there was nothing she could do to help. Most of all, she missed the loving arms of her mother and sitting in the lively company of her family. Her entire life she'd been surrounded by their comforting chatter. That was something no WhatsApp or Skype call could replace. She also felt responsible for the danger they were in, and though she had no idea how she would do so, she was determined to get them all out of Egypt so they could start a new life together.

I met Doaa for the first time in January 2015 and spent several hours in her host family's living room, drinking tea and interviewing her about her ordeal. I was struck by her determination to tell her story, and I soon realized she was entrusting me with it for two reasons—to help her and her family resettle in another country and to warn other refugees who were tempted to make the same dangerous journey. It soon became clear to me that she felt the responsibility that elder sons in Arab cultures would usually bear, that of having to take care of their families. Doaa felt that only she could change her family's destiny. By that point, she had clearly lost trust in governments to help her and faith that the culprits who had sunk the boat would be found and brought to justice. "We Syrians have no one to support us except God," she told me. "Maybe there is an interest in us, but only in words. I'm exhausted. I can't go back to my parents; my family cannot come here. I have heard so many promises, but I want to see action."

I was determined to bring her story to the world stage, but also to help her restart her life in Sweden. Her heroism had been widely recognized by the Greek press, and she had been given the annual award by the prestigious Academy of Athens a few months after being rescued. But I felt strongly that her story deserved the attention of a global audience, and I was sure it would capture their imagination.

My colleagues launched a formal process for her resettlement, unusual at that time for Greece, another EU country. But Doaa was treated as a special case—a traumatized young woman with a family at risk—and so they appealed for special consideration. There was a system in place for resettlement from countries like Egypt that hosted refugees, and given the family's precarious situation, they met UNHCR's "vulnerability" criteria. Doaa and her family's applications were linked together, and a request was made that they be resettled to the same place.

I was with Doaa at an outdoor café in Chania, Crete, in October 2015 when I received the call that the Swedish government had accepted her and her family's resettlement application and that she should be prepared to depart in a few weeks. For the first time since we had begun working on the book together, I saw a look of real joy on her face. As I ordered ice cream sundaes to celebrate, she ecstatically called her parents to relay the news.

On January 18, 2016, Hanaa, Shokri, Saja, Nawara, and Hamudi boarded a plane from Cairo to Stockholm, switching planes to the provincial city airport of Östersund. They were greeted at the airport by the Swedish officials assigned to their case and loaded into a van that would take them to their new home a few hours' drive from the airport in the tiny village of Hammerdal in the snowy northeast of Sweden. That same morning, Doaa boarded a plane from Chania to Athens, then to Copenhagen, Stockholm, and finally Östersund. When she arrived at their new home around midnight, trudging through three feet of snow to the entrance, she was shivering from cold that she had never before felt. When she knocked shyly on the front door, within seconds, Hanaa threw it open, with her arms extended toward her daughter. Shokri stood behind her, his eyes full of tears. After one and a half years, Doaa finally felt the warm embrace of her mother, and she never wanted to let go again.

Despite having lost everything that used to define them— home, community, livelihoods—refugees like Doaa refuse to lose hope. But what choices were left to Doaa and her family? To remain a refugee in Egypt, with little opportunity for education or meaningful work? To return to a war zone where the future was even bleaker and, on top of that, dangerous? Or to take a risk by taking to the sea on a so-called boat of death to seek safety and better opportunities in Europe?

For most refugees, there is nothing left to return home to. Their houses, businesses, and cities have been destroyed. Since the crisis in Syria began in 2011, fighting has progressively engulfed all regions, and the economy and services are in a state of general collapse. Half of the Syrian population (almost five million people) has been forced to flee their homes in order to save their lives. Another 6.5 million are internally displaced. Since March 2011, at least a quarter of a million Syrians have been killed in the fighting (some estimates double that number), and over one million have been injured. Life expectancy among Syrians has dropped by more than twenty years, and an estimated 13.5 million people, including 6 million children, are in need of humanitarian assistance. But half of those people in need are in hard-to-reach or besieged areas, making the delivery of aid very difficult, and in some places impossible.

At the time of publication of this book, the Syrian war rages into its sixth year, and five million refugees have made their way to neighboring countries to find shelter in bleak desert camps, makeshift dwellings, or crumbling city apartments in Lebanon, Jordan, Turkey, Egypt, and Iraq. Every day, they watch the news of their hometowns and cities being reduced to rubble and learn about the deaths of friends and loved ones, which has a profound psychological impact.

The once welcoming communities they live in are now overwhelmed with the burden of hosting so many people in need. In tiny Lebanon, a country struggling with poverty and instability, 25 percent of the population are now refugees. There are not enough schools, water systems, sanitation facilities, or shelters to support this swelling population.

After more than five years of conflict with little prospect for peace, many Syrians have now abandoned hope of ever going back to their homes. With nothing left and their places of exile under increasing strain, refugees feel compelled to travel much farther to find safe havens that would also allow them to educate their children and rebuild their lives, even if such a journey means risking death during a perilous crossing of the Mediterranean or Aegean Sea.

It took the sudden surge of Syrians arriving in Europe in 2014 and 2015 to rouse governments to pledge more support to the refugees in the region. Europe suddenly recognized that they could no longer leave Lebanon, Jordan, and Turkey without support while refugees struggled amid dire conditions. An international conference in London in January 2015 garnered unprecedented funding pledges for humanitarian organizations and host countries, as well as for educational and employment programs. A deal was struck with Turkey that offered billions of dollars to the country in exchange for help in preventing refugees from fleeing. Border fences were installed in the Balkans to block refugees that were already in Greece and to discourage others from making their way to Europe. But the financial pledges that have materialized in the wake of the conference have fallen far short of the needs of the refugees, and there is little visible improvement to their living standards.

Doaa's story is the story of millions who live in limbo waiting for asylum and watching the news of the fighting back home. It's also the story of international powers becoming entangled in regional rivalries and how they are either unable or unwilling to stop the war.

Doaa and her family are now restarting their lives in safe and generous Sweden. Doaa, Hanaa, and Shokri spend their days in Swedish classes learning the language, and Saja, Narawa, and Hamudi are enrolled in local schools. But I have to ask, why did Doaa have to risk her life, lose her fiancé, and witness the death of five hundred others to finally arrive at this place of refuge and opportunity?

What if Bassem could have been given a visa to work abroad? What if Masa and her family had been given the chance to formally unite with their other family members already in northern Europe? What if none of them had had to take that risk? What if there were a legal avenue to reach Europe from Egypt to study abroad? Why is there no massive resettlement program for Syrians—the victims of the worst war of our times? Why are the neighboring countries and communities hosting five million Syrian refugees being offered so little funding and support for infrastructure and development? And of course, the main question: Why is so little being done to stop the wars, persecution, and poverty that drive so many people to flee for the shores of Europe?

The simple truth is that refugees would not risk their lives on such a dangerous journey if they could thrive where they were. Migrants fleeing grinding poverty would not be on those boats if they could feed themselves and their children at home or in bordering host countries. Nobody would resort to spending their life savings to hire the notorious smugglers if they could apply to resettle in a safe country legally. Until these problems are addressed, people will continue to cross the sea, endangering their lives to seek asylum. No person fleeing conflict or persecution should have to die trying to reach safety.

Doaa's hope is that none of her fellow passengers on her boat will have died in vain. She is outraged that the bottom of the sea was the only place five hundred refugees, including the man she loved, could find refuge. She feels grateful to Sweden for offering her and her family asylum and a new start, but she worries for her two older sisters who are struggling with their families as refugees living in Jordan and Lebanon.

Doaa spends several hours every day in Swedish courses and one day hopes to start university and study law. With a law degree, she believes she will be able to fight for more justice.

In May 2015, Doaa traveled to Vienna, Austria, to receive the OPEC Fund for International Development's Annual Award for Development. The award committee chose Doaa for "her bravery and her determination to draw greater attention to the refugee crisis by sharing her story." The prize money will go toward furthering her education and helping other refugee shipwreck survivors. When she accepted the award, she stood before an admiring high-society crowd wearing ball gowns and tuxedos and told them, "No man wishes to end his life by taking off his life jacket. No family ever dreams of displacement. . . . These journeys take refugees from despair to death. Tonight you have given me some peace."

A Note from Doaa

In this book, I have shared my suffering with you. It is only a small glimpse of the hardship and pain that refugees around the world endure. I represent just one voice among the millions who risk their lives every day in order to live a life of dignity.

The perilous journey refugees take in order to reach safety in Europe often leads to despair and death. But we put our lives in the hands of cruel and merciless smugglers because we have no other choice. We have been confronted with the horrors of war and the indignity of losing our homes. Our only wish is to live in peace. We are not terrorists. We are human beings just like you. We have hearts that feel, yearn, love, and hurt.

Every family in my country has lost so much that they have had to rebuild their homes in their hearts. We have lost our homeland, and our dreams are all in the past. If only all the tragedies we have lived through were just a nightmare that we could wake up from.

The people responsible for the war in Syria don't care about shedding the blood of a child, tearing apart families, or destroying homes. And the world doesn't seem to mourn for all the people that have drowned in the sea during their search for sanctuary.

My fiancé, who was the love of my life, slipped out of my arms and drowned right in front of my eyes, and there was nothing I could do about it. Now, my life without him feels like a painting without any color. More than anything, I just wish he were still with me.

When I was afloat in the sea, I did my best to keep Masa and Malak alive. Over those four horrific days, they became a part of me. When I learned that precious Malak took her last breath after we were rescued, I felt like someone tore my heart out of my chest. But I do find comfort in knowing that she has made her way to heaven. A heaven where she has at last found safety, and there is no fighting or wars.

I am grateful to all of those who refuse to remain indifferent. I especially want to recognize our Egyptian friends who made my family feel welcome, the captain and crew of the *CPO Japan* who came to my rescue, the pilots who pulled us into their helicopter, the doctors on Crete who saved our lives, and my host family on Crete, who took me in and gave me the space to heal. I also want to give a special thanks to UNHCR for arranging our resettlement and to the government of Sweden for giving us a safe and promising new home.

One day, I hope to return to Syria so I can breathe again. Even if it's just for one day. That would be enough.

Author's Note

I first came across Doaa's story on the UNHCR Greece website. As head of communications for UNHCR, I am always on the lookout for distinctive accounts of survival and resilience that illustrate refugees' predicaments while also building bridges of empathy to the public. It was March 2015, and I was set to speak at a TEDx event in Thessaloniki, Greece, in May about the refugee crisis on the Mediterranean. I knew at once that Doaa's story would stir the Greek audience and resonate with people everywhere who were trying to understand what was driving thousands of refugees to risk their lives crossing the sea to Europe, pushing them even further away from their homeland after having already escaped the horrors of war.

I arranged a Skype call with my colleague in Athens, Erasmia Roumana, who had been assigned to handle Doaa and Masa's cases, to see how UNHCR could help. Erasmia interviewed Doaa after her release from the hospital to assess her needs and to let her know that she had the right to claim asylum in Greece. As Erasmia told me Doaa's story, I could tell that she was visibly shaken. Erasmia had witnessed and heard all kinds of tragic tales during her work with refugees, but no story had gripped her heart the way Doaa's did. I traveled to Crete a few weeks later to meet Doaa myself.

My communications colleagues in Athens—Ketty Kehayioylou, Stella Nanou, and Katerina Kitidi—arranged my visit and researched and translated all the coverage in the Greek media for my preparation. These articles, as well as photos and other accounts, would later prove useful for the book, despite some inaccuracies in the news reporting that became clear after cross-checking.

My colleagues Ana White and Sybella Wilkes traveled with me to Crete, and Sybella supported me throughout the entire process of scripting the story for the TED talk. I conducted my first interview with Doaa on April 21, 2015, in the living room of her host family on Crete. Doaa spoke only Arabic, and our interpreter could only translate from Arabic to Greek, so Erasmia translated the three-hour conversation from Greek to English. It soon became clear that the reports in the media had only skimmed the surface of the nightmare and struggles that Doaa had lived through in Syria and Egypt and on the Mediterranean Sea. Doaa was welcoming and warm, but also very fragile and clearly traumatized. At one point, after she relayed the details of how Bassem had drowned, I asked her if she wanted to continue. "Ask me what you want," she said. "This is my life. I live with it." Her guard was up very high at that point, but it was clear she saw us as people she could potentially trust to help her. There was one thing she wanted and that was to be resettled in Sweden along with her family members who were still back in Egypt and whom she felt responsible to protect, and she knew we were the only ones who could help her.

Doaa's host family, who took her in after her rescue and cared for her like one of their own daughters for sixteen months, was helpful in providing us access to Doaa. However, they declined to be interviewed for the book, explaining that they believed that what they did for her was "God's will," and therefore they did not deserve recognition for their generosity. That is why I am preserving their anonymity in this book. But I do want to recognize them here. They provided a place of healing, protection, and love for Doaa, and this was a very noble and beautiful deed.

The day after meeting Doaa, we traveled to Heraklion to visit the University Hospital where little Masa had been treated after her rescue, and met with Dr. Diana Fitrolaki, her supervising physician. She confirmed to me that Masa "was close to death" when she was first admitted. "We gave her glucose, liquid, oxygen," she told me. "And we sang her songs, hugged her, took her into our arms, and walked around. After two days, she started to smile. She always asked to be picked up. She wanted to be held all the time. The staff were always touching and holding her. They love all the children but had never seen a case like this before." I left the hospital that day convinced that it was not just modern medicine that had saved

Masa but the love that Dr. Fitrolaki and the University Hospital staff showered over the little girl from the moment she was admitted.

After having left the hospital, Masa was being cared for at an orphanage, the Mitera foster home in Athens. During my visit there, I spent a couple of hours playing with her and speaking to the manager and staff of Mitera. It was clear to me that the bubbly toddler who had quickly picked up the Greek language was in the best place possible to overcome her trauma and the tragic drowning of her parents and sister.

Later, at UNHCR's Athens office, I conducted a Skype interview with Mohammad Dasuqi, Masa's uncle who was living in Sweden. His wife, two children, and Masa's elder sister, Sidra, darted in and out of the frame as we spoke. Mohammad was awaiting the outcome of a legal procedure that would confirm his genetic relationship and ability to care for Masa so that he could bring her to Sweden to join her older sister and his family and so he could become her legal guardian.

That same afternoon, my colleagues arranged for one of the other survivors, Shoukri Al-Assoulli, to meet us at our Athens office. Shoukri was in a terrible state when we met with him. The Palestinian National Authority had stopped paying his small monthly stipend due to a lack of funds, and a few days before, in a park in central Athens, members of the right-wing extremist group the Golden Dawn had beaten him and a friend badly because they were foreigners. They both landed in the hospital. He was penniless and broken, and crying as he showed us a photo of the pretty pink bedroom his deceased daughter used to sleep in back in Gaza. Shoukri wanted to share his story, and we agreed that Jowan Akkash, a Syrian journalist he had befriended who was translating for us, would ask him my interview questions when the time was right. This interview, along with another session months later, when Shoukri had returned to Gaza, corroborated further details and added description of what transpired during the boat journey and during the time they struggled for survival at sea.

Once I had finally gathered enough information to write the script for my TED talk, I shared the text with the curators of TEDxThessaloniki, Katerina Biliouri and Elena Papadopoulou, who were immediately convinced that their Greek audience would be deeply moved by Doaa's story while also gaining a wider understanding of the reasons why so many refugees were dying on their shores. In the lead-up to and aftermath of the event, Katerina and Elena made special efforts to promote the talk. Bruno Giussani, TED's European director and curator of the TEDGlobal conference, also offered to review the script and provided insightful advice and helpful edits that significantly improved the shape of the script. I am also grateful to Mark Turner, who helped to make the words sing. I rehearsed the talk over and over, and my colleagues, especially Sybella Wilkes, Edith Champagne, Christopher Reardon, Alexandre St-Denis, and Médéric Droz-dit-Busset, served as patient and active audience members for rehearsals and provided lots of feedback. Speaker coach T. J. Walker supported me throughout the process, critiquing rehearsal videos and keeping me on a practice regimen. When I delivered the talk on May 23,

2015, the audience listened in rapt silence, then stood to applaud once I finished. Many were in tears. A fellow speaker and prominent Athens businessman, Alexis Pantazis, was so moved by Doaa's story that he granted her a scholarship in the name of his company.

I decided to send a link to a video of the talk to literary agent Mollie Glick, then of Foundry Media, now at CAA, who had previously reached out to me about writing a book after she had seen my first refugee-themed TED talk. "Is this a book?" I asked her. Her response was clear: "Yes!" With Mollie's passionate outreach and strong belief in the timeliness of a refugee story like Doaa's, we set to work on coming up with a proposal, and she recommended Dorothy Hearst, an experienced nonfiction editor and successful novelist, to help me with the proposal process and the writing. Mollie's assistant, Joy Fowlkes, who had brought my first TED talk to Mollie's attention, managed all the contacts in different time zones, and Foundry's Kirsten Neuhaus secured eight foreign publishers on the basis of the book proposal and is working on more.

My book ended up with Flatiron Books, a division of Macmillan. My editor, Colin Dickerman, impressed me with his interest in human stories that move, educate, and influence readers. Since then, Colin has expertly guided me throughout the writing and marketing process, keeping me to deadlines and encouraging me to write the best book that I had in me. As the manuscript entered its final stages, Flatiron editor Jasmine Faustino significantly improved the flow and form of the text with her sharp and fresh eye for style and structure. Copy editor Steve Boldt and publishing lawyer Michael Cantwell both combed through the final draft for inconsistencies and refined the text to a fine finish.

Revealing part of her story for a short TED talk was already a big deal for Doaa, but exposing entire life story in detail for a book was a frightening prospect. I was deeply convinced that telling her story would help her come to terms with the tragedy and also offer her some much-needed financial support. I was also sure that her story would give readers real insight into the Syrian war, the grueling life that refugees face in neighboring countries, and the factors that drive so many people to risk their lives to cross the Mediterranean to reach the promise of Europe. My colleague Firas Kayal, a fellow Syrian who was deeply moved by Doaa's ordeal, was instrumental in convincing Doaa and her family that the book was in their best interest and that they could trust me to write it. Doaa's instinct was to withdraw into her trauma, and Firas helped her to understand how she could help other people by telling her story to the world.

To get the level of detail I needed, it was clear that I needed to work with a collaborator who not only spoke fluent Arabic but who was also sensitive to the plight of the Syrian people. I found that person in Zahra Mackaoui, a video journalist and documentary filmmaker who had worked for UNHCR covering Syrian refugee stories from Lebanon. Zahra has always impressed me with her talent for individual storytelling while painting a wider picture and generating compassion for Syrian refugees suffering and circumstances. She quickly developed a strong relationship with Doaa and her family. Her sensitive and caring approach earned their trust and confidence. Most interviews we conducted together, though some she conducted alone when I was unable to travel—in all, the interviews add up to over seventy hours of conversations. Some sessions were so painful for Doaa that we had to break off and start again the next day. We were the only ones she had spoken to at this level of detail about what had happened, and it seemed to help Doaa to talk about it. Zahra knew how to comfort her when she felt sad and to make her laugh to lighten her mood. Over the seven months we spent working together on the research, Zahra became a dear friend and a mentor to Doaa. The transcripts she worked on, which were translated thanks to Naglaa Abdelmoneim, provided a detailed account of what had happened over Doaa's life, set vivid scenes, and captured her family's dialogue. Zahra ensured that the transcripts were complete and coherent, that the time lines were accurate, that any lapses in memory were resolved, and that the emotions of the moment were captured. She also added perceptive commentary and contributed descriptive writing that helped shape the overall narrative and helped fully develop the contours of Doaa's character.

At about the same time that I started working on the book in October 2015, the TED editorial team, led by Helen Walters and Emily McManus, published my talk on TED.com. The response was phenomenal. By the time I finished writing the book in August 2016, over 1.3 million people had viewed it, and it was subtitled in thirty languages by the talented volunteer

TED translators. I am grateful to the TED editorial team for recognizing the power of Doaa's tale and for providing the TED platform to raise awareness about the global refugee crisis.

I could not have written this book without Dorothy Hearst's masterful writing support. She taught me the ins and outs of book publishing and the art of writing in long form. She also gave me confidence when my writing felt blocked or clunky, and she steered me with tips on how to improve. She provided chapter-by-chapter polishing, and her edits and additions helped bring the scenes into more vivid focus with color and emotion.

I would also like to recognize Jane Corbin, whose seminal BBC documentary on the Daara uprising helped me set the scenes that sparked the Syrian war. Other works that served as important references were *Burning Country* by Robin Yassin-Kassab and Leila al-Shami, as well as Patrick Kingsley's *The New Odyssey*. I would also like to recognize the citizen journalists whose brave video reporting paid witness to the events that mainstream media, historians, and writers like myself refer to for helping to paint a picture of the war. Many thanks to Maher Samaan for checking the facts around the Syria chapters.

Bruno Giussani's edits and insightful suggestions improved the writing and the context throughout the process. I am also grateful to Ariane Rummery, Sybella Wilkes, Edith Champagne, Christopher Reardon, Elizabeth Tan, Yvonne Richard, and Elena Dorfman for reading the manuscript and offering so many words of encouragement. Additional thanks to Elena for the stunning portraits she took of Doaa.

I am deeply grateful to Pat Mitchell, curator of TED-Women, who linked me to the Rockefeller Center Fellowship program in Bellagio, Italy. I was awarded a one-month policy fellowship at their stunning residence on Lake Como in April 2016 that gave me the ideal environment, space, and time that I needed to write important chapters for the book. Special appreciation goes to Managing Director Pilar Palacia for her heartfelt interest in the project and for welcoming Doaa and Zahra for daily interview sessions over three days in the tranquility of the center's facilities and grounds.

In addition to Doaa's testimony, there were several interviews that were critical to the book. I am deeply grateful to Hanaa, Shokri, Saja, and Nawara for fielding all my questions and providing so much insight into their family life, Doaa as a person, and Doaa and Bassem's love story. My interviews with Doaa's sisters, Ayat in Lebanon and Asma in Jordan, gave me insight into Doaa's personality and her struggle to accept Bassem's death.

Thanks also goes to the doctor in Egypt from MSF who, while preferring to remain unnamed, gave such a moving account of not only Doaa's fragile medical condition and Bassem's poor state of health but also of their optimism and tremendous love for one another.

Special thanks also to Svante Somizlaff of Offen Group, a tanker and container ship management company in Hamburg, Germany. Doaa's rescue ship, the *CPO Japan*, is one of the tankers in its fleet. Svante was immensely helpful in tracking down Doaa's rescuers. He activated the personnel department to find the three men manning the ship that day, Captain Vladislav Akimov, Chief Mate Dmytro Zbitnyev, and Engineer Vladislavs Daleckis, transmitting their detailed written responses to my questions. These interviews corroborated the timing of the rescue and added details to the story that Doaa had been in no condition to recall, such as the decision by the captain to search for survivors even though the other merchant vessel at the scene had given up amid the poor visibility and rough seas, the point when they heard her cries, how they worked to finally reach her, the medical measures they took to care for the people they rescued, and how Malak died.

I am also grateful to the pilots John Fragkiadoukis and Antonios Kollias of the Greek Hellenic Air Force, who provided important details of their helicopter rescue of Doaa, Masa, and the other survivors in addition to providing the dramatic video they had shot as they were pulling them up to the helicopter from the ship. For them, this rescue was almost routine, but they still recall this particular incident because it involved a young woman and a baby who were so visibly on the edge of death and whose survival in the middle of the Mediterranean Sea for such a long period of time seemed miraculous.

I am sincerely grateful to Aurvasi Patel and Diane Goodman for their efforts in working with the Greek, Egyptian, and Swedish governments to get Doaa and her family resettled. Thanks to them, Doaa has renewed hope.

Big thanks to *Humans of New York* photographer Brandon

Stanton and authors Khaled Hosseini and Neil Gaiman for their endorsements and to my colleague Coco Campbell for her strong support of the project.

Although I wrote the book in my personal capacity, the then UN High Commissioner for Refugees, António Guterres, endorsed the project, believing it would serve as an important communications tool to drive empathy for refugees. I wish to underscore that most of the proceeds of this book will be donated to support refugees.

The writing process took place over a period when the refugee crisis in Europe was making daily headline news and my UNHCR workload was at an all-time high. I am so thankful to my husband, Peter, and my children, Alessi and Danny, for not just accepting that my evenings and weekends were consumed by writing the book but for cheering me along.